Advance Praise for
The Child with Autism Goes to Florida

"*Its reader-friendly format* and practical advice is invaluable. This booklet will help countless families plan the ultimate vacation."

Ayda Sanver Halker
Director of Information, Referral, and Customer Service
Autism Society of America

"*Kathy reviews the resorts,* rides, rest spots, the 'must sees,' and the 'save this for next times.' It's easy to follow ... it's so user-friendly!"

Dee Galen
Author of *Fruit, Numbers, and Questions of How Many More*

the Child with Autism

Goes to Florida

Hundreds of practical tips,
with reviews of theme parks,
rides, resorts, and more!

KATHY LABOSH

FUTURE HORIZONS INC.
Arlington, Texas

 Goes to Florida

All marketing and publishing rights guaranteed to and reserved by:

FUTURE HORIZONS INC.
721 W. Abram Street
Arlington, Texas 76013
800-489-0727
817-277-0727
817-277-2270 (fax)
E-MAIL: *info@FHautism.com*
www.FHautism.com

Book design © TLC Graphics, *www.TLCGraphics.com*
Cover by: Monica Thomas; Interior by: Erin Stark

IPublisher's Cataloging-In-Publication Data
(Prepared by The Donohue Group, Inc.)

Labosh, Kathy.
  The child with autism goes to Florida : hundreds of practical tips, with reviews of theme parks, rides, resorts, and more! / Kathy Labosh. — [2nd. ed., rev. and updated].

    p. ; cm. — (The child with autism)

  Includes index.
  ISBN: 978-1-935274-24-7

  1. Autistic children—Travel. 2. Florida—Description and travel. I. Title. II. Title: Goes to Florida

RJ506.A9 L323 2011
618.92/858/82

Printed in the United States of America

This book is dedicated to Dee Galen,
who believed in me when I was just dreaming.
I believe in you, too.
Give a big hug to Koryn & Trevor for me.

Acknowledgements

Thank you to the contributors and consultants who lent their support and expertise:

Moira Allbritton, mother of multiple children with autism, for sharing her traveling tips with me.

Roy and Cynthia Weinhold and Andrew Bonsall, for sharing their time with my family while in Florida. We all learned together.

Table of Contents

Part One:
Things To Know Before You Go

Part Two:
Getting There

Part Three:
The Universal Family
of Theme Parks and Resorts

Part Four:
The Disney Family
of Theme Parks and Resorts

Part Five:
The Anheuser-Busch Family
of Theme Parks and Resorts

Foreword

Thank you so much for your help! Your book was our "bible" at Disney. Your advice was incredibly helpful and made a world of difference in the wonderful memories we have of our first family vacation together. I had been very unsure about our visit to Disney's parks, as we have not always had great success at our local parks.

We decided to try Disney's Magic Kingdom and two water parks. After the great experience we had, we found ourselves already planning next year's trip even before we left Florida. I will definitely use your book when visiting the other parks next year! I told my husband that I liked the idea of how you had "measured" your children's progress with each visit, and I find myself wondering how my children will react next year. You were right: Disney has a special kind of magic, and it really touched our family.

I knew your book was going to be a success when I heard myself repeatedly telling my husband, "Katie said to try this. . ." and he would repeatedly respond, "And she was right," when it worked. It was almost like you were on vacation with us!

Knowing that the advice in the book came from a parent who understands the complexities involved in dealing with autism made us feel comfortable and prepared for any uncertain situations that might arise at the park. Just one example of this occurred when our son was tired, and beginning to get frustrated. My husband thought we might have to miss the parade, but I knew just what to do. We took him to Tom Sawyer's Island with a bucket of popcorn, and he sat in a rocking chair for an hour, just cooling off, while we enjoyed the parade immensely. I was silently thanking you the entire time. Without your advice, I never would have thought to try this strategy, and we would definitely have missed the parade!

So many aspects of the advice in the book were helpful to us. For example, our children *did* enjoy Blizzard Beach much more than Typhoon Lagoon, and there was definitely more to do at the Beach. I found myself saying things like, "Katie says, 'Take the child to a ride after doing what he wants for fifteen to twenty minutes. Then go back to doing what he wants.' With the Disabilities Pass, you don't have to rush, and you'll get the same things accomplished anyway, at a slower pace.'" This greatly reduced our anxiety, and as a result, the kids' anxiety was also low.

Before our trip, I thought we would go to Disney and maybe go on one ride—we went on FIFTEEN! The comfort of knowing what would be relaxing and enjoyable for our children (and what might frighten them) virtually made the decisions for us as to which rides or events to try.

As parents of children with autism, having the knowledge that let us plan for unexpected situations was an invaluable tool. The advice in your book truly looked at things from the point of view of a child with autism. This let us help our children get the most out of their experience, and enjoy it to the fullest. For that, and for helping us pile up memories for a lifetime that we will hold dear to our hearts, we thank you.

My boys are brothers, and they both have autism, but they are very different. For example, Sam loves the characters in costume, while Nick is afraid of them, but your advice worked for both of them.

Thank you for caring enough to share you experiences with us. I told my husband that I could not imagine the amount of work it took to pull all of that incredible knowledge together—but we are both very grateful that you did.

THE RAFFOUL FAMILY
George, Christina, Sam, and Nick

Preface

Some of the best times I have had with my children have been at the Florida theme parks. While the rest of the crowds hurried by, Nicky and I have leaned tranquilly over the bridges to Cinderella's Castle playing "Pooh Sticks," watching leaves and sticks idle by on the lazy streams. We do not do that much anymore, and I miss those times, but I am proud of his progress. Each year we return is like a developmental measuring stick, where I get to see my children enjoy rides and exhibits that intimidated them before. Even my low-functioning child, Nicky, now struts about with confidence.

The sensory stimulation at the parks can have a wonderful effect on our children. A look of awe fills Nicky's face when we visit the parks at night. To get the most out of your theme park vacations, get your children used to new sensory experiences at local amusement parks. *The Child with Autism at Home and in the Community* contains a chapter on desensitizing your child to the crowds, the sounds, and the smells of amusement parks. Doing this now will pay off with longer, happier stays at theme parks later.

For many people, a visit to Florida is not complete without a stay in one of the many resorts associated with the theme parks. There are many benefits associated with these stays, including transportation to the parks and extended park hours. We usually stay in a timeshare, but I made a special trip to Florida in order to stay in a resort and visit many of the others.

All the resorts are of high caliber and fine for the typical family. I was looking specifically for how breakable the furniture was, as well as potential hazards regarding water, fire, balconies, and the ease of losing a child. This may seem like an overly negative approach to take. Not all children with autism have all these issues. However, if your child has a particular issue, such as running away, you may want to choose a resort that is not surrounded by lush vegetation.

After each family of parks, I have listed the resorts associated with that park. This is not a comprehensive list, as I was not able to visit every resort, and some were viewed on the Internet. There may be something glaring that I would have caught if I had been able to personally visit each one. I cannot anticipate everything a child with autism might do. My goal is to provide relevant information in order to help you make the best lodging choice for your family. This information is not meant to be a substitute for your own judgment or diligent care over your children.

I wish you the best of everything on your trip. If you see a boy with sandy brown hair bouncing like Tigger and yelling, "Eee!" that would be Nicky. Come on over and say "Hi!" Whether you see us or not, I want to thank you for making me a part of your trip. It has been my aspiration to be a guide your family can trust.

KATHY LABOSH

Part One

Things To Know Before You Go

~

The Florida theme parks are grouped into
three families: Universal, Disney, and Anheuser-Busch.
You might think they are competitors,
but they are not. They market to different customers,
usually found within the same family.
The diversity and sheer quantity of rides
at these parks guarantees that the whole
family will be happy to come
back year after year.

Chapter 1

Transportation and Parking

Trust me—you don't want to skip this section. These may seem like minor issues, but they can make or break your trip.

- Plan to have at least two means of transportation back and forth to the parks. This will allow the family to split up if the child with autism needs a break. This way, the family can also view different attractions without the child and caregiver pacing outside while other family members visit their favorite rides.

- Stay at a resort that has transportation to the different parks. The caretaker and the child with autism should use a car if possible, and the rest of the family can use the shuttles.

- Ride the shuttle during off hours. It can be standing-room-only during the opening and closing rushes.

- Rent a second car if you drove down and are staying at a hotel with inadequate or no shuttle service.

- Buy your Disney tickets from AAA; then you are entitled to an AAA Diamond parking pass. The AAA spaces are within easy walking distance of the main gate.

- Ask the parking attendant where the Diamond parking is. There are different colored lines to follow at each park.

- Make a note of where you are parked, especially if you are in the regular parking. Also make a note of the make, model, and license plate of your rental car. You are in for a long walk if all you can recall is that it's a silver, mid-size car.

- Place something distinctive in the front and/or back window of your car. It will help you locate your car quickly.

- Push the automatic horn button found on many key chains. However, be aware that, at closing time, many other people will be doing the same thing. You may be surrounded by honking cars!

- Look carefully at your parking-lot character. Daisy and Minnie may be close friends, but they are at opposite ends of the parking lot.

- Board the tram toward the back. The loudspeaker isn't as loud there.

- Sit with your child to the inside, with your arm around him. Have him look at the row numbers or cartoon characters as you go.

- Universal Studios and Islands of Adventure share a parking garage. There are no Diamond passes, but you can pay extra for preferred parking that is closer. I have not found it to be a difficult walk from any part of the garage.

Chapter 2

Tickets and Searches

These tips should cut down on the time the child with autism has to wait in line.

- Buy your tickets ahead of time. They are available at AAA, online, and also at the resorts.

- Get tickets that include the park-hopping feature. This will give you the freedom to visit other parks if your child finishes a park early.

- Add Disney Quest and the water park features onto the pass. Individually, they can be very expensive, and it's money wasted if they stay only briefly before wanting to go home.

- Buy an annual pass if you intend to go every year. Take your second vacation before the fifty-two weeks are up. This will save you money.

- Place your belongings in a fanny pack. Don't forget this guide! This will leave both your hands free to tend to the child, and keep your cell phone, tickets, keys, and money safe. These items often fall out of regular pants or shorts pockets.

- Bring a change of clothes for the child, in case he gets wet or has an accident.

- Put those clothes in a backpack. There are lockers inside the park where it can be stored.
- Have one person carry the bags to be searched through the search area. This will speed the child and the caregiver through.
- Meet at a designated place inside the park to regroup. I have suggested peaceful places just inside the parks where you can calm a flustered child.

Chapter 3

Theme Park Touring and Ride Tips

Proceed to Guest Relations to pick up a Disabilities Pass for the child. Bring a letter from your doctor stating that the child has autism and would have difficulty waiting in line. Ask for the pass even if you forgot the note. Many parks no longer require it.

- Check with Guest Services at your resort. They may be able to get you a pass even before you leave for the parks.

- Get the pass once. All the related parks accept the same pass. You will need to get a different pass only when you enter a new family of parks.

- Take your time. With the pass, you do not need to hurry to each ride. Rushing just raises a child's anxiety level.

- Let the child lead you to what he finds interesting. Many of the "calm down" places I have found in the parks are from times that Nicky and I spent playing with the fountain water, or looking for sticks among the trees.

- Take the child to a ride after doing what he wants for fifteen to twenty minutes. Then go back to doing what he wants. You will end up going on about the same number of rides as the rest of the group.

- Associate splashing water with fun by taking your child to local water parks before putting him on the theme-park water rides.

- Put your child in a swimsuit before putting him on a water ride. This will let him know it's time to get wet. Also, if he wants to get out of his wet clothes, you'll have his dry clothes to put back on.

- Avoid scary rides. We know that everything is special effects. The child does not have the concept of "pretend." He will believe that a dinosaur is really chasing him!

- Do not try to reason with your child. He relies heavily on his senses and will have difficulty disbelieving them.

- Give a scared child something concrete to say or do to counter-act his fears. The reasoning portion of the brain is impaired, so just tell him to say, "God help me," or "Go away!" to whatever is frightening.

- Don't use walkie-talkies to communicate with each other unless they have many channels. The lower channels are crowded because so many other people will be using them. It can be very difficult to get through to your group. Use cell phones if you have them.

- Relax and have fun. You do not have to see everything in every park. There is always next year!

Chapter 4

Lost Children

Ninety-nine percent of the time, you are checking on what your child is doing. The other one percent of the time, you lose him. These tips will help you and others locate him quickly.

- Make a dog tag printed with your child's name, the word "autism," and your cell phone number.

- Attach the tag to the interior laces of your child's shoe or some other place easily seen but difficult to remove. Children with autism usually will not tolerate having anything around their neck.

- Dress your child in distinctive clothing. There are hundreds of brown-haired boys wearing green shirts, but only one with the word **LABOSH** on the back.

- Bring a recent photo of your child to the park with you.

- Think of what attracts your child. If he likes fountains, check the nearest ones.

- Alert the park quickly, so they can check people leaving the park. It might not be a case of abduction. The child could simply have grown tired of the park, and has headed back to the car. The assumption of the park staff would be that he is with a nearby family group, unless they are on the lookout for that particular child.

- Being prepared decreases worry. It does not increase the likelihood of losing the child.
- Remember that even Mary and Joseph lost Jesus on a family trip. It can happen to anyone. Having a child prone to running away means that you are better prepared than most to deal with the situation.

Chapter 5

Kennedy Space Center

If you are coming to tour the Center, I do not think there will be a problem if your child can do museums. If you are coming to see a launch, leave the child at home with a responsible adult. The launch is very loud and the traffic is horrendous. You may be stuck in traffic for hours. It is worth seeing—just not with a screaming child in the car with nowhere to go.

Chapter 6

Beaches

There are a lot of beaches in Florida. I have been to several, mostly near Tampa and Panama City. My comments are therefore general and not specific to a particular beach. Whichever beach you plan to visit, be sure to find out when school starts or ends in the area where you are hoping to go. Over spring break and post-graduation days, these places are packed with fun-seeking young adults. Plan your vacation days accordingly. If you plan around those times, the beaches will be less crowded.

There are five kinds of beaches:

- *Driving Beaches.* There are beaches in Florida that you can drive on. This is usually limited to a particular section of the beach or to certain times. A child might run straight for the water, not looking for a car. So be sure to stay at a beach that does not allow driving.

- *Shell Beaches.* These beaches are usually not as crowded as other beaches, but you will need to wear swim shoes on your feet because there are many broken shells in the sand. Many of these beaches are on the west side of Florida and they have beautiful sunset views.

- *Sand Beaches.* They still have some shells, but they are usually partially buried in the sand. This makes for a more enjoyable walk on the beach, but as a result the beaches are usually more crowded. Beaches near smaller towns may be less crowded but are usually not as well maintained.

- *Natural Beaches.* These beaches found in state parks can be beautiful. Wildlife shares the park with you. On a camping trip, I encountered a skunk, egrets, pelicans, and an armadillo. But there are some animals you definitely do NOT want to run into. Alligators and crocodiles are a very real threat, especially to children and pets. Keeps kids close when exploring undeveloped areas, and avoid being in or around the water at dawn and dusk. Ask the camp ranger or campground manager about specific places to avoid or other precautions you can take.

- *Family Fun Beaches.* These beaches are usually well maintained and they have a variety of activities available, like miniature golf and amusement rides.

Chapter 7

Hurricanes

My advice stems from staying in Florida about five miles from Punta Gorda where Hurricane Charlie made landfall. Normally we drive down to Florida, but that particular time we flew into Tampa Bay and rented a car. Tampa Bay, with its airport right by the water, was projected to be the landing point of Hurricane Charlie. But it made a sudden right turn into Punta Gorda.

If you are inland, especially in the Orlando area, stay put. You might get a power outage and some downed vegetation, but the hurricane's fury is reserved for the coast. Your hotel or resort staff should be able to take care of you.

Otherwise ...

- Call the airport to see if you can get out on an earlier flight. Be sure to let the airline employee know that someone in your party must be sitting next to your child.

- If you cannot get a flight out, call inland hotels and resorts and book a room that you can stay in. The further inland you get the better.

- Check your address book. See if you have any relatives or friends who live in the Florida area and may be able to take your family in for the night. We stayed with some friends from New Jersey who had retired to Sarasota.

- Find out where the emergency shelters are in the area where you are staying, and what kinds of accommodations they provide during emergencies. There are never any guarantees, but you can get a general idea of what to expect in terms of aid and supplies.

- The special needs shelters are often for people in wheelchairs or who need oxygen and nursing care. You need to make sure that your child would not be a danger to those people if you go there.

- If you decide to drive home, call and make reservations for where you are going to spend the night ahead of time. Hotels up and down the I-95 corridor may be full. You might find yourself taking every exit and stopping at every hotel trying to find a vacancy into the wee hours of the night.

- If you are trapped in a storm surge area, go as high as you can in the house. Bring a saw or hammer to provide an emergency way out if you are stuck.

- If you are stuck in the hurricane area, but are out of danger from the storm surge, get in a closet or some interior room to shield you from blowing objects. A flipped over couch could be a shelter as a last resort.

- If you are in a safe place, listen to the TV or radio for only a few minutes at a time. Excessively watching the storm coverage could add to your stress and even lead you to do something foolish.

- The weather preceding the hurricane is usually beautiful. Do not waste that time by squeezing in more activities. Use it to prepare.

Part Two

Getting There

~

Any trip to Florida begins in your own home.
Several decisions that you make there will have an
impact on your trip to Florida. Should we go by plane,
train or automobile? Should we rent a car when
we get there? How can I prep the kids for the trip?

Chapter 8

Check for Package Deals

If you are going only to Disney, the folks there are amazing. They have wonderful package deals—they will arrange the flights, car rentals, meal plans, restaurant reservations, you name it. You get a final price and that's what you pay.

AAA also offers booking services. If you book through them, you can have access to the special AAA parking at the Disney Parks. These spaces are usually right next to the handicapped section so they can save you from having to park far away and wait for parking-lot trolleys.

Chapter 9

Traveling by Airplane

Flying has never been cheap or easy for special-needs families. New security measures—along with the fear and paranoia they induce—do not make the trip any easier. Unfortunately, there have been families who have gotten booted off of airplanes because their child with autism was acting up. It is best to prepare your child and the airline staff ahead of time.

- Contact the airline and ask what their policy is regarding children with disabilities.

- Bring a letter from your pediatrician explaining your child's condition. (This may come in handy at other places as well.)

- Have your pediatrician write a prescription for a sedative that you can give the child on an as-needed basis. But be aware that sleeping on the plane could mean being up all night.

- Bring sleeping pills for you and other adults, in case you need them.

- Fill a small carry-on with some of his favorite toys or comfort items (double check that these items are permitted on the plane).

- Mark all suitcases with something that makes it easily identifiable at the baggage claim. Waiting for luggage with a tired, cranky child is not fun.

- If you are going to the Disney Resorts, they can arrange your flights, have your luggage picked up at the airport and delivered to your room, and take your family to the resort by bus. They will reverse the process going home.

- Make your seating arrangements ahead of time. Have a family member sit beside the child but also in front of the child. Airlines can be resistant to this because they like family groups in a row. However if you inform them that your child has autism and may be kicking the seat in front of him for the whole trip, they are happy to help you.

- Allow generous layovers, so that you are not running with the child to your next connection.

- Designate one person to be the "mule" (carrying all the bags) and the other person to be the caregiver. This should help the caregiver and child get through security quicker.

- If one of the adults needs to go the restroom, the adults need to split the mule's load. It is very difficult to follow a child with autism *and* carry all of the bags at the same time. (Keep in mind that airport officials no longer allow you to leave luggage unattended.)

- At home, practice together taking shoes off, walking through a door, and putting them back on.

- Practice the arms-out, legs-spread pose they sometimes ask you to do in the event you have to go through advanced screening.

- Start out at a small airport, so that security clearance lines are shorter. This will give them a practice run, before they have to deal with Orlando security coming home.

- Ask if there is a line for handicapped persons, as that line will be shorter. The staff assigned to that line should be more sensitive to special needs as well.

- Be sure to empty the child's pockets of calculators, portable video games, and other items before going through the metal detector, otherwise you are headed to advanced screening.

- Be among the first to board the plane, so the child does not have the wait in the aisle when people are stowing baggage. That way the child will not have as many people to stare at coming in.

- Seat the child by the window. The other seats can block the view of the other passengers boarding.

- Put the tray table down and spread out toys for the child to play with before takeoff.

- Bring a small, personal DVD player, if allowed, and quietly play a movie the child enjoys.

- After exiting the plane, have one person get the rental car (the caregiver) while the mule gathers the entire family's luggage. This will cut down on the time spent at the airport.

Chapter 10

Rental Cars

These cars are very expensive in Orlando. The rental car companies are going to tell you one price and neglect to tell you all of the added taxes and fees that comprise a large part of the bill. If you go the rental-car route, you really should pay for the added insurance. Even if you are a good driver, there are people from all over the world who do not know where they are going, converging on a few places. A trip does not go by without a close call.

- Figure out if you actually need a rental car. Many of the resorts have shuttles to the airports and around their own family of parks. If you are planning on spending the whole time at Disney, you could use their shuttles.

- A rental car is good if you want to be able to split the family and go home "now" if the child is stressed.

- A rental car is good if you are staying at a time share and want to drive to the grocery store, or get the child's favorite meal from a nearby restaurant.

- A rental car is good if you want to see Disney and Universal or Sea World. It gives you more flexibility.

- A rental car is good if you want to go to church or visit family while you are there.

- Bring a lot of change with you, as there are toll roads going from the airport to Disney and Universal. The rental car companies have an option of paying the tolls for you. That is very expensive. Sometimes their "plan" is that you drive through the toll booths, setting off the alarms and they will pay for the tickets when they come in. Others will give you an electronic pass. Bring a lot of change and say, "No thank you."

- Go on the computer and map out the routes that you will take ahead of time with directions. They can help you avoid some of the tolls and it will help with the transition period.

Chapter 11

Traveling by Car

This is actually our preferred method of travel, but then, our kids love riding in a car.

- Make a schedule book that has pockets or folders for each day you are going to be there. Fill each day's pocket with a brochure of the park that you will be visiting, and let the child read through it in the car.

- Have your child choose the toys that he wants to bring in the car with him.

- Create separate snack packs for each day of the trip.

- Give some candy to the child AFTER he gets back into the care during a rest stop. They can be resistant to getting back in the car if it is a long trip. This gives them incentive.

- Bring along a personal DVD player with some favorite movies.

- Allow some time in your schedule for the child to let off some steam in the hotel room or at the pool. They can be very active after they leave the car, so allow them to expend that pent-up energy.

Chapter 12

Lodging

Pick up some food at a drive-through just before you check in. Eating food in the car will give the kids something to do while waiting. They will also be in a better mood if they're not hungry.

- Stay at a hotel with a pool. The child needs a reward for sitting all day in the car and it will burn off some energy.

- If this is an overnight stop, pack one bag with everyone's clothes for the next day. This eliminates taking everyone's luggage out of the car for a single night's stay.

- Bring Goodnights® underwear for the kids to sleep in. Even potty-trained kids can have accidents when stressed or exhausted.

- Take tables and chairs off the balcony. With no fear, it can seem like a reasonable way to leave the room.

- If your child is a runner, bring a barbell to place in front of the door. Fire laws require that people be able to leave easily. The deadbolt only works to keep people from coming in, not going out.

- Check below the balcony before leaving to make sure nothing has been dropped by little hands.

- If your child likes baths, put him in the bath while you are moving into your main hotel room. It keeps him occupied and away from all of the unpacking. (Obviously, do this only if you feel the child is capable of taking a bath with minimal supervision.)

- Put the child's favorite things on their assigned bed. Have the child help you put their things in a drawer, if they are able.

Chapter 13

The Auto-Train

Since the early 1970s, Amtrak has had a special nonstop train that starts in Lorton, Virginia, just below Washington, D.C., and it takes you *and* your car all the way to Sanford, Florida, just a little bit north of Orlando. This way you can move around, eat, and sleep more comfortably during the 900-mile trip. I have never tried it personally, but I know people who swear by it. You might want to look into it if long car rides and airports do not appeal to you or your family.

Passengers have to check in their cars an hour or two before the train departs, so you can pack up the car for your stay in Florida and pack separate bags for the 18-hour train trip. You can reserve your own "bedroom" with a private bathroom and comfortable seats that convert into beds at night. Or you can reserve a smaller "roomette" that accommodates one or two people and is near public restrooms. Coach seats are the most economical option, but those may not work well for some families. Meals are included in the price. Be sure to peruse the menus online, as you will probably need to supplement the meals. There is a movie for the kids in the evening. The Amtrak website says that special accommodations are available for families with special needs, so be sure to ask about those.

Whichever way you choose to get there, good luck, have fun, and make some great memories along the way!

Part Three

The Universal Family of Theme Parks

Universal Studios and Islands of Adventure
reflect the rich film heritage of the studio.
Universal Pictures has a treasure trove of horror movies.
The marquee movie rides in the park are for
thrill-seekers looking to be scared by special effects
and daredevil rides. You may think there is nothing
for a child with autism in these parks,
but you will find that is not true.
Behind the billboard attractions are a host
of rides and attractions that your
children will enjoy.

Chapter 14

Islands of Adventure

Port of Entry

The entrance is filled with shops and restaurants, and packed with people who are entering the park. Go straight until you reach the lake if your child needs a place to settle down. Most people will go either to the right toward Seuss Landing, or to the left toward Marvel Super Hero Island.

Seuss Landing

This is a whimsical area for small children. I have very few caveats about anything in this area. There is a little place for your child to settle down, by the store named Cats, Hats, and Things.

- *If I Ran the Zoo:* The children should enjoy this play area. The water squirts can be avoided if your child has water issues. Come back later if it is too crowded.

- *The High in the Sky Seuss Trolley Train Ride!*: This is a good air ride for the children. It can be a little noisy while going through the buildings, but it provides a wonderful overview of Seuss Landing.

- *The Cat in the Hat:* This is a good first ride that takes you through the story of *The Cat in the Hat.* The car swings from side to side and sometimes all the way around. Being familiar with the story will increase everyone's enjoyment of the ride.

- *One Fish, Two Fish, Red Fish, Blue Fish:* It looks like a typical ride where you go up in the air in little fish, but fountains of water will squirt at you. Have your child watch it first, so that he will be prepared for the squirts.

- *Caro-Seuss-El:* Low-functioning children often have trouble with merry-go-rounds. The loud music, the up-and-down motion, and the spinning are sometimes too much sensory input for a low-functioning child. Start with a stationary seat. This eliminates the up-and-down motion. Stand on the park side of the child if he is on a moving animal. If he is upset, that is the direction he will try to escape in.

The Lost Continent

There is good scenery in The Lost Continent. Behind the Mythos restaurant there are quiet places to take the child away from the crowds for a little exploring. Watching the waterfalls can be very exciting for him.

- *Poseidon's Fury:* This is too intense even for a high-functioning child. There are spectral images, loud noises, explosions, and angry gods warring with each other.

- *The Mystic Fountain:* This fountain talks to people who go near it. Your child will probably be a little wary, but I think he could have fun with this. Decide whether to tell your child ahead of time.

- *The Eighth Voyage of Sinbad:* This is a stunt show. There are loud explosions, fire, and daredevil acts as Sinbad triumphs over evil. Low-functioning children have problems staying seated during the show, and are likely to be disturbed by the special effects. A prepared, high-functioning child who is savvy about shows should be able to handle it.

The Wizarding World of Harry Potter

The whole area is an accurate reproduction of the Village of Hogsmeade and Hogwarts. Fans of Harry Potter may enjoy visiting many of the famous places, even if the rides are too intense. Caveat: Go during the off-season. This area gets packed with 15–20 minute waits to get into the stores!

- *Ollivanders Famous Wand Shop:* There are two ways to visit this store. The shortest line is to visit just the wand store. There is a long line which lets you visit the wizard. One child in the room is selected for a wand. Mishaps and mayhem occur until the "correct" wand is selected. Afterward, you enter the wand shop through a different entrance. This can be scary, but a high-functioning Harry Potter fan would probably love it.

- *Dervish and Banges:* This shop has the snarling book, *The Monster Book of Monsters,* in a cage.

- *Harry Potter and the Forbidden Journey:* The line weaves through many of the Hogwarts' classrooms. The ride itself is a next-generation simulation ride that rotates and pivots your seat as you "fly" with Harry and his friends through some of their scariest film adventures. This is very scary and for ride-savvy, high-functioning children only.

- *Dragon Challenge:* It is possible for a child with autism to learn to love roller coasters. He could become addicted to the sensory input, and he needs to be introduced to them slowly. Only take a high-functioning roller coaster addict on this one!

- *Flight of the Hippogriff:* This is a pretty good coaster, considering its size. It would not be the first roller coaster you should put your child with autism on, but it would be a good second coaster, raising the excitement level over the simple child's coaster.

- *The Three Broomsticks:* This restaurant has a very efficient system for feeding crowds. You line up to place your orders and are then sent to one of many stations for pickup of your meals. The best part is that an employee then finds you an open table to sit at. This method saves the whole family from standing in line and you do not have to wander around with trays, and children in tow.

Jurassic Park

Children and dinosaurs just seem to go together. There are many exhibits and activities that should interest your child. The trails in front of the Jurassic Park Discovery Center are good for getting away from the crowds with your child.

- *Jurassic Park Discovery Center:* There are many interactive exhibits that the children can play with. I had to drag my younger son out of there, because I wanted to see more than just this exhibit.

- *Jurassic Park River Adventure:* This ride is too scary for children with autism. Your river tour of Jurassic Park goes terribly off course, and you find yourself amid incredibly realistic, angry dinosaurs. There is a splash at the end.

- *Camp Jurassic:* A children's play area for them to run around and burn off some of that boundless energy.

- *Pteranodon Flyers:* I cannot recommend this ride. You fly through the air on front-and-back tandem seats, swinging as you go. Your child is in front of you, beyond your reach. He cannot see you. If he panics, your voice is the only thing that can calm him down—and that might not be enough.

Toon Lagoon

This is a fun place to explore. Comic conversation balloons fill the area, giving plenty of opportunities for funny photos. There are good paths behind Popeye's boat (called Me Ship, the Olive) for you to walk with your child. Change your child into a swimsuit if you are going on any of the rides in this area. This will mentally prepare him for getting very wet.

- *Dudley Do-Right's Ripsaw Falls:* A high functioning child should be okay with this ride, provided he is prepared ahead of time. There is a brief period of darkness and a series of drops and splashes throughout the ride, including a big one at the end. You will get soaked. Ponchos are available for purchase in front of the ride's entrance.

- *Me Ship, the Olive:* A low-functioning child should enjoy climbing all over Popeye's ship. There is an opportunity to shoot water at the people on the *Bilge Rat* ride below.

- *Popeye & Bluto's Bilge Rat Barges:* Only for children who associate getting splashed with having fun. Dress your child in his swimsuit or have another set of clothes for him to change into. You will get wet all over! Place your shoes and socks in the center storage compartment; otherwise, you will walk around in squishy sneakers all day. I laughed from the beginning to the end of this ride, but I also had to go into the bathroom afterward and literally wring out my clothing. They have ponchos for sale, but they won't help you much.

Marvel Super Hero Island

This area has some marvelous rides for teenagers and adults, but not much for children with autism. Only Storm Force Accelatron would be appropriate for most children with autism. I recommend taking turns watching the child with autism so each adult can go on these rides. Children with sound sensitivities may be bothered by the blaring rock music. You can explore the quieter water's edge if you are waiting for a member of your party to return.

- *The Amazing Adventures of Spider-Man:* Amazing is correct. This 3-D ride takes you into a battle between Spider-Man and the Evildoers. It all occurs inches from your face, and is too intense for children with autism.

- *Doctor Doom's Fearfall:* You are lifted up high and then dropped up and down like a yo-yo. It's too intense for children with autism (and the author).

- *Storm Force Accelatron:* This is like the spinning-cups ride, but it has a cooler design. If your child loves getting dizzy, he will love this ride.

- *Incredible Hulk Coaster:* This ride is too intense for most children with autism. A high-functioning roller coaster addict would love it.

Chapter 15

Universal Studios

The billboard attractions in this park are too intense for most children with autism, but the park has several excellent children's sections, outdoor shows, and wonderful scenery that a child with autism would enjoy.

The more intense rides have single-rider lanes that move very quickly. You can take turns watching the child, or they also have baby-swap areas where both parents and the child enter the waiting line. The one parent goes on the ride while the other parent holds the child in the baby-swap area. When the first parent is done with the ride, they switch places. The caregiver then boards with no further waiting.

Production Central

- *Jimmy Neutron's Nicktoon Blast:* This is a rough simulator ride that rockets you through the Nickelodeon cartoon sets with the characters. The rough action can induce feelings of nausea, but this can be avoided by sitting in the stationary seats in the front row. Being familiar with the cartoon should increase the level of enjoyment.

- *Hollywood Rip Ride Rockit:* This intense roller coaster allows you to choose a song to hear during your ride. If you do not choose a song, a song will be chosen for you. If the child does not have a favorite, I recommend Gloria Gaynor's "I Will Survive," to avoid some of the louder, harsher music. Recommended for coaster addicts only.

- *Shrek 4-D:* Watch *Shrek* before viewing this sequel. The child needs to be familiar with the story and the characters in order to make sense of what they are watching. Many children with autism have trouble with 3-D shows. They don't like the feel of glasses on their head or seeing the characters come off the screen to within inches of their face. Watching without the glasses is difficult, because then the characters appear blurry or double. The fourth dimension is touch. You will feel wind, water, and tickles. You can request seats that don't move or have the touch feature. You will also smell some odors. Don't go on this attraction if anyone is afraid of spiders, because they do play on that fear. Create a social story for a high-functioning child to prepare him for what he is about to see and feel.

New York

- *Twister ... Ride It Out:* This would be too intense for a child with autism. You see, hear, and feel what a tornado is like, close up.

- *The Blues Brothers:* Another good outdoor show. You can see them from a distance and hear them from even further away. Get as close as your child will let you.

- *Disaster!:* This attraction has four stages. The first stage has a live person interacting with a hologram of a crazy producer of disaster films. The second stage has people from the audience acting in front of a green screen. During the third stage, a child with autism may get scared. Everyone boards a tram which is then subjected to a series of disasters involving fire, water, earthquakes, and collisions. People are encouraged to scream, panic, and overact for the cameras. During the fourth stage, when the tram returns, you get to view your finished film. If you want to do the attraction, but are concerned about the third stage, ask if the child and a caregiver could stay at the tram platform. It will only take a few minutes for the tram to return.

- *Revenge of the Mummy:* Utter darkness, fireballs, spectral demons, warrior mummies, and bugs are guaranteed to undo years of therapy. This is too intense for children with autism, and for the author, too.

San Francisco / Amity

- *Beetlejuice's Graveyard Revue:* This attraction features extremely loud music and explosions—too much for a child with autism. You can stand a block away if you want to hear the show.

- *Jaws:* This is a good intermediate-level ride to raise the excitement level for a child who is now ride-savvy. Prepare a social story for a high-functioning child before putting him on the ride. Tell him that a mechanical shark is going to come out of the water and tug on the boat. Then the shark will go back into the water and he will be okay. Make a game out of looking for the shark.

World Expo

- *Men in Black—Alien Attack:* This is perfect for a high-functioning child who loves video games, because the ride is one big video game. As an adult, I loved this ride, but the aliens may be too realistic for some children with autism. Prepare them ahead of time.

- *The Simpsons Ride:* This next-generation simulator ride follows the Simpsons through a carnival, as Sideshow Bob tries to kill them. There is comic book intensity to the action that feels realistic as your car pivots and rocks. If your high-functioning child is familiar with the Simpsons and is comfortable with simulator rides, go for it. Otherwise wait until your child is more ride-savvy. Not recommended for low-functioning children.

Woody Woodpecker's Kidzone

- *Animal Actors On Location!:* A show that even a low-functioning child would enjoy, if he will sit through it. Exiting is easy if he wants to leave mid-show.

- *A Day in the Park with Barney:* It is one thing to see him on the television, but it is entirely different for these children to see him up close. You can try it, but even if they are avid Barney fans, they may be scared of the "real" Barney.

- *Curious George Goes to Town:* The children should love this interactive playground!

- *Woody Woodpecker's Nuthouse Coaster:* A school-age child who likes sensory stimulation could try this with a parent. Have the child watch the ride a couple of times first. Ask him if he wants to go on it. Have him count how many seconds the ride takes. Tell him if he gets scared to start counting and it will be over soon. Hopefully, he will enjoy it.

- *Fievel's Playground:* Children should enjoy this play area.

- *E.T. Adventure:* At the beginning of this ride you are being chased by the army, and this may be too intense for some low-functioning children. Higher-functioning children should be told that it's going to be okay, and that the car is not going to hit them.

Hollywood

- *Universal Orlando's Horror Make-Up Show:* A good-natured live show with some practical jokes thrown in to startle the audience. This is not for a child who is easily frightened or startled. A montage of clips from horror movies is shown.

- *Terminator 2: 3-D Battle Across Time:* Highly recommended for adults, but this is too intense for anyone with autism. The 3-D effects are unbelievably realistic!

- *Lucy—A Tribute:* This walk-through exhibit is full of memorabilia and pictures from the life of Lucille Ball. A child with autism would probably get little out of it, but there should not be a problem taking him with you if you are interested.

- *King Kong 360 3-D:* This one wasn't open yet at the time of my last visit, but the promised "visceral special effects," including violent 3-D dinosaurs, an angry King Kong, and the illusion of falling into a giant chasm, sound too intense for children with autism.

Chapter 16

Universal Resorts

The Universal theme parks have three resorts associated with them: The Hard Rock Hotel, Portofino Bay, and Royal Pacific. I visited the Hard Rock Hotel and Portofino Bay; I reviewed the Royal Pacific over the Internet.

Staying at one of the resorts entitles you to the following privileges: your hotel key acts as the Universal Express ride access pass, allowing you to bypass regular lines at select rides and attractions; there is on-site transportation to each of the Universal Parks, as well as to Sea World and Wet 'n' Wild; you receive priority seating at restaurants; and purchases made at the parks can be delivered to your room. Guest services can also provide babysitting service referrals. Room refrigerators are available for a fee, but if you let them know that you need one for a medical reason, such as a special diet, the fee may be waived.

- *The Hard Rock Hotel:* One of the features I most appreciate at the Universal hotels is that their pool areas are gated. The sight lines around the outdoor sand-beach pool with a water slide are not always clear, but the child is limited as to how far he can go. A negative is that there is an underwater music system that may bother a sound-sensitive child. There is another pool area without these features. The other potential issue with this resort is the hard rock music that plays throughout. It could bother a child with sound sensitivities. The furniture in the room appears to be sturdy. There are some lamps that may catch a child's interest. Call housekeeping, and they will remove them if you think they may be a temptation for your child.

- *Loews Portofino Bay Hotel:* This resort has three seasonally heated pools that are fenced in. Some of the pools have sight-line issues, but there is a pool with clear sight lines in every direction. The furniture is sturdy and beautiful. The only drawback is that the layout is very confusing. Getting from Guest Services to the pool area required me to make several turns in the hallways, go up and down steps, and cross piazzas. I relied heavily on the signs posted on the walls. This is something that a child with autism would not be able to do. I hope it is easier for the guests who are staying in the rooms.

- *Loews Royal Pacific Resort:* This resort was viewed over the Internet. I am not sure whether the pool area is fenced or not. If it is like the other Universal resorts, it is. Lush vegetation surrounds the resort and pool areas, which creates sight-line issues if you are searching for a lost child. The furniture is beautiful, but the beds have posts that could be snapped. The entertainment involves fire at the Wantilan Luau.

Part Four

The Disney Family of Theme Parks

The Disney family of theme parks
and resorts has scenery, rides, and accommodations
geared to delight even the youngest visitor.

Most of the rides are fine; however,
some rides and shows highlight the Disney
villains with extreme sensory stimulation that
may be too intense for children with autism.
Please read the review of each attraction
before deciding whether to place
a low-functioning child on the ride.

Chapter 17

Magic Kingdom

Main Street

Be sure to visit the Kodak exhibit directly across from City Hall. There is a little garden with a fountain to the right, and this is a good spot for a child to relax.

- *Walt Disney World Railroad:* The disabilities section is near the front of the train. Unfortunately, there is a very noisy water fill-up when you get to Mickey's Toon-town Fair. Either plan to get off there, or sit toward the back of the train, where the noise is not an issue.
- *City Hall:* This is where Guest Services is located. Stop here to get your disabilities pass. The pass is good in all Disney parks.
- *The Town Square Theater:* Disney's Photo Pass center and Tony's Town Square Restaurant are housed in this building.

Adventureland

There are wonderful shady spots over the bridges into Adventureland and the bridge to Frontierland. You can gather small sticks and fallen leaves to play Pooh Sticks from the bridges.

- *Swiss Family Treehouse:* A good attraction that even a low-functioning child can enjoy. You climb the tree, look at the rooms, and climb back down. A low-functioning child may push the people in front of him, or attempt to pass them. Most people understand if you explain that the child has autism.

- *Shrunken Ned's Junior Jungle Boats:* Buy tokens to maneuver tiny boats around obstacles in a pond. A low-functioning child might enjoy watching the action. A child who likes video games might want to give it a try.

- *The Pirates League:* Your child can get a pirate makeover (priced separately). Many children with autism can have issues with makeup and costuming.

- *The Magic Carpets of Aladdin:* A good first ride that gets you off the ground. Watch out for the camel; he spits at passers-by!

- *The Enchanted Tiki Room—Under New Management:* This is not the Tiki Room that you remember from when you were growing up. It starts out the same way, with the French birds, but it is then taken over by Iago, the parrot from Aladdin. It gets very dark and scary, and my child was terrified during the show. It is difficult to get out once the show starts.

- *Jungle Cruise:* A good first ride for your child. There is a cave near the end, but he should be able to handle it.

- *Pirates of the Caribbean:* This ride is dark, both in lighting and in theme. These are *not* jolly pirates. This is a realistic depiction of how pirates actually were. There is a scene of a woman being sold into slavery, and a sea battle that is noisy. Your boat goes over a medium dip. You should be able to take a high-functioning child with you if you want to go.

Frontierland

A stressed child will enjoy running along the boardwalk paths that border a corner of the lake. Much time has been spent examining the water below. The best place for a child who is stressed is Tom Sawyer's Island, where he can run to his heart's content.

- *Walt Disney World Railroad:* Frontierland has a less-crowded station than others for boarding the train.

- *Splash Mountain:* This enchanting water ride provides a whimsical re-telling of the tale of Brer Rabbit. It is a good first flume ride for a high-functioning child. You can see a big water drop from the outside, but there are a series of little drops inside that trick you into believing that it's going to be the big one. (Hint: vultures are not a good sign!) The little drops on the inside might convince the child that he can handle the larger drop at the end. Let him know ahead of time that he might get wet. Take this ride at night for a fabulous view of Cinderella's castle.

- *Big Thunder Mountain Railroad:* This wild coaster is too intense for most children with autism. It starts in the dark with spiders and bats looking at you with glowing eyes, and then it is up and down, in and out of the mountain with tight turns. There are slow periods when it seems like the ride is ending, but it only takes off again. My concern is that a frightened child might be anxious enough to disembark during a slow period.

- *Tom Sawyer Island:* A low-functioning child should love the island, if you can get him onto the raft to get over there. Put him near the edge of the raft, facing the water. He will be less conscious of the other people on the raft this way. The island itself is full of trails, forts, bridges, and play areas for the child to explore. You and your kids will get a workout. I had to force my child to leave, because I wanted to see other attractions.

- *Country Bear Jamboree:* Try it and see. There are different bears singing country songs of their own making. A few familiar talents lend their voices. You can easily leave through a side curtain if your child doesn't like it.

- *Frontierland Shootin' Arcade:* Try it and see. A low-functioning child might like watching, or he might find it too noisy. Explain to a high-functioning child that this is like a video game without the computer.

Liberty Square

Liberty Square has only the lakefront to explore. If your child is stressed, take a short walk around the lake to Frontierland.

- *Hall of Presidents:* A high-functioning child should be able to sit through the show. A child who likes to collect facts or who knows the presidents should really enjoy it!

- *Liberty Square Riverboat:* Children enjoy the room to run around and the sensory feel of the air on their faces. Just keep them away from the whistle. It is loud, and hot water droplets may fall on them from the condensing steam.

- *The Haunted Mansion:* Although this is a pretty light-hearted ride, there are some aspects of it that could disturb a child with autism. The floor of a room drops slowly, which could be disconcerting. The child may also be concerned about the ghosts if they can't discern between fantasy and reality. This should be okay for a high-functioning child who is a veteran of many rides. Prepare him for what is going to happen.

Fantasyland

Near Cinderella's castle is a little fountain, and Nicky enjoyed long spells of splashing in it. Many people use the fountain as a photo opportunity, but no one ever disturbed us. There is also a water cascade near the Toontown Fair side of the castle, and it mesmerized Nicky as well.

- *It's a Small World:* This is a wonderful ride for low-functioning children. It can be a little loud when boarding, but overall not a problem.

- *Peter Pan's Flight:* A good ride for a low-functioning child with some ride experience. The flight over London requires a small level of trust in the ride.

- *Mickey's PhilharMagic:* Children with autism typically do not do very well in 3-D shows. They do not like wearing glasses, and if they do wear them, the characters seem to be literally "in their face." Other sensory input includes loud noises, wind, and sprinkles of water. There is nothing inherently scary about the show itself, so you can try it with a high-functioning child who has few sensitivities. Warn him ahead of time that the characters are going to appear to come off the screen.

- *Prince Charming Regal Carrousel:* Low functioning children with autism take a long time to get used to merry-go-rounds. The music is loud, the horses go up and down, while part of the world is spinning and part seems constant. Start with a stationary horse in case your child wants to exit the ride.

- *Dumbo the Flying Elephant:* A great first ride for low-functioning child with autism. A parent should accompany the child.

- *Snow White's Scary Adventures:* This ride may be too scary for children with autism, as they might be bothered by the wicked witch, the darkness, and the scary trees.

- *Bibbidi Bobbidi Boutique:* A beauty salon is located inside Cinderella's Castle for little girls who wish to be made over into a princess (priced separately). Many children with autism do not like make-up on their faces.

- *The Many Adventures of Winnie the Pooh:* This is a wonderful ride through the story of *Winnie the Pooh and the Honey Tree.* Your child should like it, especially if he is familiar with the characters and the story.

- *Mad Tea Party:* If your child likes to spin and get dizzy, this is the ride for him!

- *Coming Soon:* The Little Mermaid: Ariel's Undersea Adventure.

Mickey's Toontown Fair

There is a back walkway to Tomorrowland that goes by the Indy Speedway. It's the least crowded part of this park, which is packed with little children.

- *Minnie's Country House:* You and your child can walk through Minnie's house and see how it is furnished.

- *Toontown Hall of Fame Tent:* Meet characters and get their autograph.

- *Judge's Tent:* Meet Mickey Mouse and get his autograph.

- *Mickey's Country House:* You and your child walk through Mickey's house and see how it is furnished.

- *Donald's Boat:* This is a fun play area that even low-functioning children enjoy, if they can tolerate being around other children.

- *The Barnstormer at Goofy's Wiseacre Farm:* This is a good first roller coaster. It's like the bigger coasters, but the ride ends so quickly your child won't have much time to react.

Tomorrowland

Here you will find good places for quiet exploration at the water cascades by Cosmic Ray's Starlight Café.

- *Monsters Inc. Laugh Floor* (previously *The Timekeeper*): This attraction features animated characters telling jokes—including some submitted by the audience. It's okay for high-functioning children, but the twenty-minute show is probably too much for the low-functioning child.

- *Tomorrowland Speedway:* This ride might be difficult for a child with sensory issues, as it's very noisy and smells of gasoline.

- *Tomorrowland Arcade:* This is a great place for children who like video games.

- *Space Mountain:* This roller coaster in the dark is too instense for children with autism. Use the Tomorrowland Transit Authority to let the children see the beautiful, star-filled interior without having to take the roller coaster ride.

- *Astro Orbiter:* This ride is located high above Tomorrowland. It should be fun for a high-functioning child who doesn't have an issue with heights.

- *Tomorrowland Transit Authority PeopleMover:* A wonderful first ride for a child with autism. It's a slow, easy, monorail ride that lets you glimpse inside the other Tomorrowland attractions-including another look at the beautiful, star-filled interior of Space Mountain.

- *Walt Disney's Carousel of Progress:* Your child must be able to sit for fifteen minutes, while the auditorium rotates around the building. You will view an American family from the turn of the twentieth century to the present.

- *Buzz Lightyear's Space Ranger Spin:* This ride is one big video game! You shoot various cartoon aliens with a laser gun. A low-functioning child might enjoy it even if he isn't able to aim or shoot. Make sure he doesn't aim the laser gun at his own eyes— or anyone else's!

- *Stitch's Great Escape:* This ride is too intense for any child with autism. There are periods of utter darkness, with loud noises as well as liquid and tactile stimulation. If your child becomes distraught, there's no easy way out.

- *Wishes Nighttime Spectacular:* This is the best fireworks show of all the parks for a child with autism. The fireworks form geometric shapes and patterns. Watch from the bridge to Tomorrowland for a great view of the pyrotechnics and Tinkerbell's flight.

Chapter 18

Disney's Hollywood Studios
(formerly Disney–MGM Studios)

This is a small, densely packed park. Just about every square inch is filled with people looking at shops or on their way to attractions. One of the few good places to calm a child who is stressed is between the Prime Time 50s Café and the Indiana Jones Stunt Spectacular, or you could try visiting a shop.

To enjoy this park, your child must be able to sit through a 15–20 minute show. If he's not able to do that, I suggest you visit another park, because just about everything appropriate for a small child here is a show. If your child is high-functioning, there are a number of rides and attractions that will appeal to him.

- *Sounds Dangerous:* This show includes seven minutes of complete darkness—you literally won't be able to see your hand in front of your face. The noises are not scary, but I think some children with autism may not have the language skills to follow the story line.

- *Indiana Jones Epic Stunt Spectacular:* Visit this attraction only if your child can tolerate loud noises, and will not be prone to imitating the stunts he observes.

- *The American Idol Experience:* This attraction is very true to the American Idol show. In fact, winners get a golden ticket to audition for the real show. There is loud music, singing, clapping, cheering, and booing the "Simon" judge. A high-functioning child may enjoy it if they can handle the sensory issues.

- *Star Tours:* This rough simulation ride takes you through space and several famous Star Wars fight scenes. This may be too intense even for a high-functioning child. However, if he wants to experience this ride, and you feel he can handle it, reassure him that the battle scenes are not real, and that he will be safe.

- *ATAS Hall of Fame Plaza:* It may be interesting to walk around.

- *Jedi Training Academy:* Kids are chosen from the audience to learn light-saber skills with Darth Vader.

- *High School Musical 2:* This show takes place around a large hat. Expect crowds!

- *Jim Henson's Muppet Vision 3-D:* Children with autism often have trouble with 3-D shows. They don't like to wear the glasses, and they don't like it when the characters come zooming "off the screen" right in front of their faces. The humor is gentle, but the show gets very loud at the end, with explosions. Debris appears to be flying your way. Be sure to prepare your child beforehand if you intend to go.

- *Honey, I Shrunk the Kids Movie Set Adventure:* A low-functioning child should like this playground if it's not crowded. Memorize what your child is wearing, as children often disappear from view as they wander around—you'll need to be certain you are following the correct child!

- *Studio Backlot Tour:* This is too intense for most children with autism, who tend to take everything they see literally. The special effects in this tour will most likely be too scary for them.

- *Journey into Narnia: Prince Caspian:* The audience stands in a circular set from the show and view film clips. Children will enjoy this, especially if they are familiar with the movie. You get to see some of the costumes and the props used in the movie. Okay for low-functioning children.

- *Walt Disney—One Man's Dream:* This is an interesting history of the Disney family. However, most of it will be beyond your child's comprehension, and he may not want to sit through the entire show.

- *Voyage of the Little Mermaid:* This is a shortened theatric version of the movie. Be sure to familiarize your child with the story so the scary parts will not be a surprise. Better yet, watch the movie with him before you go to Florida!

- *The Magic of Disney Animation:* This is a studio tour where you meet an animator and get a glimpse of what Disney is working on next. A high-functioning child may find this fascinating; in any case, he should be fine here.

- *Playhouse Disney:* The characters from ABC's Playhouse Disney show up and perform. There are hundreds of small children sitting on the floor who are actively encouraged to scream with excitement. If you still want to go, use the Fast Pass lane to be one of the first people inside. Head to the front and sit on the floor. The rest of the children will be behind your child and out of his main line of vision. The characters on the stage may be partially obscured, but he can always stand when he can't see something. If you can't find a seat at the front, sit at the end of an aisle for easier exiting if needed.

- *The Great Movie Ride:* This is too intense for children with autism. It takes you through many of the great movies, including gangster movies and Alien.

- *Toy Story Mania:* This ride is one big video game where the car occupants play carnival games for points. Two-handed coordination is needed to aim the shooter and pull the string. Low-functioning children could enjoy this ride even if they cannot shoot.

- *Beauty and the Beast:* This is a shortened Broadway version of the show. A child capable of sitting through a show should do fine.

- *Rock 'n' Roller Coaster:* This ride is a lot of fun for adults, but is too intense for children with autism. The exception to this is the roller coaster addict. Your coaster limousine rockets through Los Angeles at very high speeds, trying to get you to the show on time. The music of Aerosmith pounds in the background.

- *The Twilight Zone Tower of Terror:* Definitely too intense for children with autism. Scary effects include darkness, ghosts, and a thirteen-floor elevator plunge.

- *Lights, Motors, Action Extreme Stunt Show:* This show includes pyrotechnics and precision stunts. It's too loud and probably too intense for most children with autism.

- *Fantasmic Fireworks Display:* This show is too intense for most children with autism. Mickey's beautiful dream becomes a nightmare in which all the villains from Disney's movies try to harm him. There are some wonderful special effects using sheets of water, but the explosions (and there are plenty of them), scary music, voices, and pictures might frighten your child. The special effects using fire are especially intense.

Chapter 19

Animal Kingdom

This is an excellent park for children with autism. Small, quiet areas abound throughout the park, giving the low-functioning child plenty of places to explore. ***Do not skip this park!***

The Oasis

The Oasis is directly in front of you when you enter Animal Kingdom. Its trails are wonderful places to take the children to settle them down. There is a stream, a small waterfall, and animals and birds to watch. The crowds usually flow to either side of this oasis, leaving you with a cozy feeling of seclusion.

- *Camp Minnie-Mickey:* This wonderful section of the park is easily missed. Coming from the Oasis, take a left when you reach the Tree of Life. The road to Camp Minnie-Mickey is between the Island Mercantile and the Pizzafari. There is a great place to meet characters in the huts across from the Lion King Theater.

- *Festival of the Lion King:* A child familiar with the movie, *The Lion King,* may be disconcerted when the show doesn't follow the story line and the songs are sung in a different order. Warn your child ahead of time. This show is a circus spectacle, where the characters from the movie celebrate Simba with a song and acrobatics. It is spectacular and should not be missed if you can help it! A low-functioning child might have a hard time sitting through the entire show.

Discovery Island

The area surrounding the Tree of Life is teeming with people going from one section of the park to another. Watch parade times, or you may be caught in a crowd, with no way off the island! If this happens, head for the Discovery Island Trails behind the Tree of Life for the duration of the parade. The Character Landing on Discovery Island is a good place to meet the Pooh characters, although the lines can be long. It could be worth the wait if your children are Pooh fans.

- *The Tree of Life:* This is the visual centerpiece of the park. This massive tree has more than 325 animals carved into it. On the main route around the tree, there is really no good place to stand undisturbed and look at the tree. Throngs of people cross Discovery Island to get to other parts of the park. The best places to view the tree are from the Discovery Island Trails and the line to get into the "It's Tough to Be a Bug!" show.

- *It's Tough to Be a Bug!:* This is not recommended for children with autism. The auditorium is underneath the Tree of Life, and it feels as though you are in an animal's den, with the earth and the roots of the tree surrounding you. Shows with 3-D images are usually difficult for children with autism. They don't like to wear the glasses, and dislike the characters coming off the screen and stopping only inches from their face. These characters are bugs and, with special effects, you can see, hear, smell, and feel them. This sensory stimulation is too intense for children who do not understand the concept of "pretend."

- *Discovery Island Trails:* There are lovely trails around the Tree of Life, where you can see animals as well as check out the tree. The trails behind the tree are good for getting away from the crowds. If you are on the right-hand side of the tree, be careful—you may suddenly find yourself caught up in the rush of people leaving the It's Tough to Be a Bug! Show.

Africa

Everything in the Africa section of the park is highly recommended foe children with autism. It's a great place to see animals, either on a self-guided walking tour through the Pangani Forest Trail, or by riding on a safari truck with Kilimanjaro Safaris. Be sure to bring your camera—you can turn your photos into great animal flashcards for your children to use at a later date.

- *Kilimanjaro Safaris:* The hardest part of this attraction is the wait. Your Disabilities Pass will get you in the Fast Pass lane, but this doesn't mean you will have instant access to boarding. Expect a five- to ten-minute wait, depending on how busy they are. This is not long, unless your child is agitated the whole time, and it is worth the wait. The trail that your bus takes can be a little bumpy, but your child should be able to handle it.

- *Pangani Forest Exploration Trail:* Set your own pace as you follow the trail through the forest and view birds and animals along the way. Trails give the children a feeling of control in a place where most of the rides control them. It can be a nice break for them.

Rafiki's Planet Watch

This area of the park can be reached only by the Wildlife Express Train that leaves from Africa. It's dedicated to conservation efforts, and contains the only petting zoo in the park.

- *Wildlife Express Train:* This old-fashioned train shuttles between Africa and Rafiki's Planet Watch every five to seven minutes. The train is different from most in that the seats run the length of the car and face outward. You will pass animal holding pens and see animal while traveling to the Planet Watch Area.

- *Habitat Habit!:* This is a short trail connecting the train station to the Conservation Station. Cotton-top Tamarin monkeys and information on conservation dot the pathway.

- *Conservation Station:* Here's another exhibit to explore at your own pace. It offers information about animal habitats, research, and animal husbandry.

- *Affection Section:* Children with autism usually ignore the animals, but you can take their hand and have them stroke the animals. Antibiotic cleanser is available. Take pictures of the animals to turn into flashcards later.

Asia

This is the newest section of the park, and it has a wonderful, self-guided tour through a jungle setting.

- *Finding Nemo: The Musical* (replaces *Tarzan Rocks*): This show is wonderful, but you do have to line up about 45 minutes before the start of the show. There is a little Nemo that shows up in different bubbles to keep the kids interested. The show follows the movie, with wonderful costumes and neat special effects. It's great for a high-functioning child who can sit through the show.

- *Expedition Everest—Legend of the Forbidden Mountain:* This is a wonderful roller coaster, but too intense for most children with autism. At times you are going backwards in complete darkness! Yeti sightings, as well!

- *Flights of Wonder:* A high-functioning child should enjoy this show. A low-functioning child could also enjoy it, if he is able to sit through it, and is not skittish about the birds in flight.

- *Kali River Rapids:* A round raft, seating 10-12 people, floats down a stream of swirling, turbulent water. There are some drops in the ride, but none of them are major. Some people on the ride will get soaked, while others won't get as wet. There is no way to plan your seating. A soaked child may want to strip off his clothes. You can purchase ponchos by the entrance, or— better yet—change into swimwear ahead of time.

- *Maharajah Jungle Trek:* This is another excellent trail where you can set your own pace. Photograph the wild animals and birds to make flashcards later. *Highly recommended!*

Dinoland U.S.A.

I have mixed feelings about this area. There is a prehistoric radio station that can be very loud. We have been on visits when my children wouldn't enter the Dinorama carnival area because of the noise.

- *The Boneyard:* I highly recommend this large play area for children. Be sure to cross over the walking bridge to the other half, which contains a large sandpit for digging dinosaur bones. It's often quieter there, and not as crowded, either. Using the bridge is the only way to access this area.

- *Fossil Fun Games:* These are carnival-type games, with a dinosaur twist. As long as the music from a neighboring rock station is tolerable, your children may be interested.

- *Primeval Whirl:* This ride is much too rough. The cars move slowly, but then unexpectedly whip quickly around hairpin turns, sending the occupants slamming against the side, or against the ridge that separates the occupants. You feel beaten up by the time the ride is over. I personally received multiple bruises as a result of this ride. Not recommended, especially for children with physical coordination issues and/or a tendency to bruise easily.

- *TriceraTop Spin:* This is a good ride, especially for children who love to spin. Unfortunately, it is right across from the radio station. Noise levels may preclude your child from entering the area.

- *Dino-Sue:* An outdoor replica of a T-Rex dinosaur skeleton.

- *DINOSAUR:* Not recommended for children with autism. This very realistic ride takes you back to just before a comet hits the Earth. It is very dark, and strobe lights illuminate dinosaurs that are close to you, and at times, deafening. Children with autism could be traumatized because of their difficulty with the concept of "pretend."

- *Meet Lucky the Dinosaur:* A free-moving, animatronic dinosaur that talks to the kids. I did not personally review this, but you can treat it as you would a character meeting.

Chapter 20

Epcot

This large park is divided into two sections: Future World and the World Showcase. Each section is filled with interesting exhibits and architecture. The Disney personnel were especially helpful to me when I needed help to bypass certain parts of an exhibit. Do not be afraid or embarrassed to ask for help. The staff truly wants you and your family to have the best time ever at their parks.

Future World

- *Leave a Legacy:* This is a good place to settle down a stressed child. Cool fountains provide entertainment. My children loved running around the stone slabs covered by images of visitors. Take the opportunity to add your picture to the monuments.

- *Spaceship Earth:* This slow-moving ride takes you through the history of communication and has only a few sensory issues. The ride is dark, and only the displays are illuminated. It can get noisy when you enter the 20th century and a myriad of voices are heard at the same time. The ride back down reminded me of a computer game. Things are so low-key that even a low-functioning child should like this ride. It is usually crowded early in the day, so try to fit it in later, when it is less crowded.

- *Universe of Energy—Ellen's Energy Adventure:* A 45-minute show is too long for a low-functioning child. At the beginning, you enter a crowded room and listen to Ellen DeGeneres and Bill Nye, the Science Guy. It is funny and interesting if your child can comprehend the language. The audience's seating is separated into several sections, and you travel *en masse* through the attraction. The section on dinosaurs could be scary. A high-functioning child should enjoy this attraction.

- *Mission: SPACE:* Feel the intense G-forces a body experiences during a rocket lift-off. It is turbulent, and some people experience nausea after this ride. Your child might feel sick and scared. (NOTE: It now has a milder "green team" option that does not involve the spinning. In both versions, you are enclosed in a small dark area with visuals showing imminent peril. You can opt out of the ride before boarding and go instead to an area with video games.)

- *Test Track:* You learn about the various tests a car goes through, and then you get into a car that replicates those tests. You hit some high speeds in your convertible. It could be too intense for a low-functioning child. My only reservation about a high-functioning child is whether you think he might try to imitate this at home, in your car. If you're not worried about that, it's a really great ride!

- *Innoventions:* These buildings are packed with many interactive exhibits. Take the child through; he is bound to find something that interests him.

The Living Seas

- *The Seas with Nemo and Friends:* This is a very gentle ride in a clam shell where you and characters from the movie search for Nemo. This attraction is fine for low-functioning children.

- *Turtle Talk with Crush:* This attraction has very gentle humor and is easy to exit. It is fine for even low-functioning children.

- *Bruce's Sub House:* This play area lets children explore a sunken submarine. Good for low-functioning children.

- Aquariums and interactive exhibits comprise the rest of the attraction.

The Wonders of Life

This building is now being renovated.

The Land

This building has four attractions, as well as shops.

- *Living with the Land:* This is suitable for high- and low-functioning children. There is a brief rumble of thunder at the beginning, but I doubt that it would bother anyone.

- *Circle of Life:* The show about humans' relationship with the land is fine, although a low-functioning child might not be able to sit through it.

- *Soarin':* This is wonderful. You are strapped into a chair and raised high in the air. You seem to be soaring over the landscapes of California. It's a great ride for a high-functioning child who will not try to get out of his chair.

Imagination

This can be a difficult area for children with autism. It's easy to get sensory overload.

- *Journey into Imagination with Figment:* Not recommended for children with sensory issues. It explores the five senses by assaulting them with loud bangs and offensive smells.

- *ImageWorks—The Kodak "What If" Lab:* Try different things and see if any appeal to your child.

World Showcase

This section of the park is wonderful for children with autism. There are many scenic nooks and crannies to explore, and also some rides. But the buildings, shops, and exhibits are the main draw.

- *Mexico:* Inside you will find some shops, the restaurant "San Angel Inn," and an attraction called *Gran Fiesta Tour with the Three Caballeros* (previously named *El Rio de Tiempo*). This boat ride takes you on a journey through the history of Mexico. The ride itself should be fine for a child with autism. Be aware that the boat stops and sits in line to be off-loaded. Some children may try to disembark when the boat stops, instead of waiting for the proper time.

- *Norway:* This attraction has several features that a child with autism would enjoy, and it's worth the visit. The Stave Church is modeled after a church in Norway. Children will enjoy peeking into the church, and there is even a Viking vessel behind it for the children to climb on. A boat ride called Maelstrom could be too frightening for low-functioning children. There is also an up-to-five-minute wait on a platform at the end of the ride, before the passengers can enter a show. Once the doors open, you can pass right through without even viewing the show, but the wait until the doors open can seem a very long time to a low-functioning child.

- *China:* This is an interesting exhibit to look through. A high-functioning child might enjoy the stunningly beautiful Circle Vision 360-degree film.

- *The Outpost:* This African outpost offers refreshments, drum shows, and storytellers.

- *Germany:* This is a collection of German shops and a restaurant. By the path there is a wonderful, miniature railroad that the children should enjoy.

- *Italy:* Here you will find a collection of shops and restaurants, but it is not a quiet place, as many tourists pose in front of it. At times, there are also "living statues" that are intriguing.

- *U.S.A.* This is a good place to get food for the children. A high-functioning child might like "The American Adventure," where Ben Franklin and Mark Twain present the history of America through animatronics. This show runs too long for most low-functioning children.

- *Japan:* This area is beautiful to look at. The Matsuriza play traditional drum songs that are thrilling. Check for show times.

- *Morocco:* Children and adults will enjoy exploring the shops and restaurants of this Middle-Eastern marketplace.

- *France:* There are shops and a restaurant. Be sure to see "Impressions de France." Sit on the left-hand side in case you have to leave early. This eighteen-minute film shows the gorgeous scenery of France and is set to music. Stay as long as your child will let you.

- *United Kingdom:* Again, there are shops and a restaurant.

- *Canada:* This area has some flowing water that the children may enjoy. The show, "O' Canada," is in circle vision. It is very good, and they have eliminated the odd-angled shots that were disconcerting to some. High-functioning children should be fine. For a low-functioning child, your stay will depend on how tolerant he is of shows.

- *IllumiNations: Reflections of Earth:* This is a fireworks show that children should enjoy. A globe in the center of the lagoon acts as a screen for pictures from around the world. The fireworks are wonderful. China is a good viewing place. The Canada side of the lagoon tends to be more crowded.

Chapter 21

Other Disney Areas

There are other areas of Walt Disney World that are often visited by guests, but they are not really considered major theme parks. This booklet will cover the two water parks, Blizzard Beach and Typhoon Lagoon, and the shopping area, Downtown Disney. There are additional areas not reviewed, including a miniature golf course, sports arena, and other attractions.

Blizzard Beach

This is the better of the two water parks for children with autism. Two children's areas provide smaller versions of the adult-sized attractions. Tike's Peak is for younger children, and Ski Patrol Training Camp is especially for teens.

- *Summit Plummet:* The tallest, fastest water slide in the United States. The rider hits speeds of 55 miles per hour during an almost vertical drop. It is actually okay if you close your eyes and pray for mercy. Seriously, if you close your eyes and keep your body still, the only sensory input your mind receives is that the board behind you is moving. That illusion is shattered if you open your eyes. Remember this if you reach the top and want to chicken out!

- *Slush Gusher:* On this water ride, you hit speeds of 35 miles per hour while sliding over several dips. The rider is briefly airborne after going over the second dip.

- *Teamboat Springs:* This family rafting ride is 1400 feet long. There are twists, turns, and drops, none of which are severe. Make sure you take them on this ride if you intend to go on the Kali River Rapids in the Animal Kingdom or Popeye and Bluto's Bilge Rat Ride at Islands of Adventure.

- *Chair Lift:* There is an enclosed car on the ride, but be wary of bringing your child up to the top of the hill on the chairlift seats. There are also steps up the hill. It's only for a high-functioning child whom you can trust on the chairlift.

- *Toboggan Racers.* Grab a special mat and pick a lane. When the lanes are full, everyone races to the bottom. Speeding headfirst down the hill is exhilarating. Many people rate this as their favorite ride.

- *Snow Stormers:* The twisting and turning fun on this flume ride mimics the path of a slalom skier.

- *Downhill Double Dipper:* This is another racing ride, but this time it's on inner tubes. Your time results are posted—a feature that children with autism may particularly enjoy!

- *Melt-Away Bay:* The waves at this beach vary from calm to six feet high. Keep non-swimmers close to shore and put floatation devices on them. The beach has rough concrete underneath.

- *Runoff Rapids*: This tubing ride has double tubes available, which allow you to introduce your child to tubing while being there to assure him that he is all right.

- *Cross Country Creek:* This lazy river circles the park, with many stops along the way. Instead of walking, you can float on your inner tube to the next section of the park. The waterfalls under Mt. Gushmore will leave you soaked. If you want to avoid the waterfalls, get out before Mt. Gushmore, and re-enter just after the waterfalls. You could also get off your tube and guide your child's tube around the waterfalls. It's not easy, but it's doable.

- *Ski Patrol Training Camp:* This is an excellent place to take young children over the toddler age. There are small tube runs, water slides, a T-bar drop, and an iceberg-hopping course. Your child should love this section of the park, and it will also prepare him for the adult-sized attractions.

- *Tike's Peak:* Here is still another great kids' area for smaller children. It has a mini-Mt. Gushmore, racer slides, tube slide, and a snow castle fountain. There is a wonderful area with picnic tables and chairs for parents who want to relax while watching their kids.

Typhoon Lagoon

Your child should enjoy Typhoon Lagoon, if he is already familiar with water parks. Typhoon Lagoon has a strict height limit on their young children's area. It is designed for children between the ages of two and six. There are no intermediate rides. It may be hard to coax a child onto the adult-sized slides if they have never been on one before. I recommend that you go to Blizzard Beach if this is your child's first visit to a water park.

- *Surf Pool:* Here you will find a large beach area with waves that vary from calm to six feet high. Keep non-swimmers close to shore, and be sure to have a flotation device on them. The beach itself is rough concrete. Consider wearing beach (water) shoes.

- *Shark Reef:* This is a saltwater aquarium for snorkeling. Your child should be able to swim, and to tolerate a mask and snorkel. My kids have never been able to do it. They are more interested in splashing around the Surf Pool.

- *Humunga Kowabunga:* These water slides are enclosed, and it is extremely difficult to get a child with autism to go down them. I would suggest the Storm Slides instead.

- *Mayday, Gang Plank, and Keelhaul Falls:* Three twisting and intertwining inner tube runs take you quickly down the mountain. At the time we were there, they had only single inner tubes, so your child must be able to do this on his own.

- *Storm Slides:* Like the Mayday, Gangplank, and Keelhaul slides, these are three twisting and intertwining slides, but they are not enclosed. Children with autism will be much more comfortable in these slides than in the enclosed ones.

- *Castaway Creek:* This is a lazy inner-tube ride that lets you drift slowly around the park. There are areas where water squirts and falls on you, which could bother a child with autism. Help steer your child away from those areas if you can.

- *Sandy White Beach:* Here you will find a good area to spread out and relax while watching the Surf Pool.

- *Ketchakiddee Creek:* This is a play area for young children, ages two to six. Height requirements are enforced. It contains many miniature slides, waterfalls, and other attractions.

Downtown Disney

Downtown Disney is divided into three sections: The Marketplace, the West Side, and Pleasure Island. Pleasure Island will not be covered, because age requirements to enter the nightclubs preclude children with autism.

The Marketplace

There are many shops and restaurants in the Marketplace. I will cover just a few that are of particular interest.

- *The Rainforest Café:* A high-functioning child may love eating here. Be warned, though, as there are thunderstorms that occur in the indoor rainforest. You do not get wet, but if your child is afraid of storms, the sounds may bother him. Some jungle animatronics roar and some beat their chests. The elephants sound their trumpets. There is a flaming dessert called "The Volcano" that the waiters carry around the restaurant. A low-functioning child may be over-stimulated, and unable to handle the wait.

- *T-Rex Café:* Similar to the Rainforest Café, except that the animatronics are not jungle animals but dinosaurs that roar. Towards the front of the gift shop is a large sandbox where children can dig for dinosaur bones.

- *RIDEMAKERZ:* This store lets children build their own radio-controlled vehicles.

- *Bibbidi Bobbidi Boutique:* A beauty salon where little girls can get a princess makeover. Many children with autism do not like make-up on their faces.

- *McDonald's:* A place for kids to chow down on their familiar favorites.

- *LEGO Imagination Center:* There are LEGO statues, including a sea serpent sitting in the water. Outside, LEGO tables provide opportunities for play.

- *Pooh Corner:* A store with nothing but Pooh merchandise. Be sure to stop here if your child is a Pooh fan!

- *Once Upon a Toy:* A great toy store with water fountains outside.

The West Side

This is the family entertainment side of Downtown Disney. I will be reviewing only the entertainment places, and not the food establishments. House of Blues, Planet Hollywood, and Bongos Cuban Café are geared toward older teens or adults.

- *AMC 24 Theatre Complex:* Current movies show late into the evening.

- *Cirque du Soleil—La Nouba:* This is a beautiful show, but difficult to explain to a child with autism. It is like a painting by Salvador Dali, come to life! Everything is surreal and dreamlike, and the acrobatics are incredible. Explain to an older, high-functioning child that the people are going to be wearing odd costumes, stand in different places, and do really neat things just to look pretty. There is really no other explanation.

- *DisneyQuest Indoor Interactive Theme Park:* This place is full of interactive video and virtual reality games. Do NOT take the "up" elevator; ask to use the stairs. The elevator goes completely dark and is followed by strobe lights, loud noises, and the spectral image of a genie. This could frighten a child with autism. The elevator is fine when you are going down. There are simple, non-violent video games on the fourth floor to the left of the bakery. The raft ride, Astroblaster, and the Creative Works are possibilities on other floors. Other games will depend on your child. I recommend that you do not put them in a situation where they would be fighting "enemies" or "aliens."

- *Goofy's Candy Co.:* There is an unbelievable array of colored M&M's and jellybeans in this shop. If you have a sweet tooth, don't miss this store!

- *Magnetron Magnetz:* Your child may find this shop interesting, and it's worth taking a look at to see if he likes it.

Chapter 22

Disney Resorts

Disney has a huge variety of themed resorts for every budget and taste. They are divided into five categories: value, moderate, deluxe, vacation club, cabins, and campgrounds. There is sure to be a resort that is perfect for your family. But the most exciting features of the Disney resorts are the benefits that come with staying there.

- *Extra Magic Hours:* Each day, a different park is open extra hours—only for the guests of the Walt Disney World Resorts. This allows you to visit the park when it is less crowded.

- *Magical Express Service:* This includes luggage pick-up at the airport, and transportation of your family by an air-conditioned, themed bus to your resort. The whole process is reversed going home. No standing around waiting for your luggage.

- *Transportation:* Free shuttle service to and from all the parks in your resort, including bus, water taxi, and monorail.

- *Dining Plan:* Pay for your meals all at once. This entitles you to meals and snacks at over one hundred selected Walt Disney World restaurants and eateries.

The Value Resorts

These resorts are built for young families. The restaurants are all food courts, with take-out containers that you can bring back to your room. Pizza delivery is also available. The exterior decorations are on a grand scale. The pools are not fenced in.

- *All-Star Sports Resort:* The court areas are made to look like sports fields with football helmets, surfboards, and other giant sports objects lining the buildings. The furniture is sturdy. The pool is seasonally heated, and has great sight lines. There are no significant bodies of water, only some small retaining pools.

- *All-Star Music Resort:* The court areas are lined with giant musical instruments. Music plays softly at the main check-in, as it does in all the resorts. You won't need to worry about noise issues. The furniture is sturdy. The pool is seasonally heated and has great sight lines. There are no significant bodies of water, only some small retaining pools.

- *All-Star Movies Resort:* The court areas are lined with four-story high Disney characters, such as Woody from *Toy Story,* and the dogs from *101 Dalmations.* Prepare your child for what he will see there. The entrances from the parking area do not have these characters, so you can enter your building without seeing them if your child is intimidated. The furniture is sturdy. The pool is seasonally heated and has great sight lines. There are no significant bodies of water, only some small retaining pools.

- *Pop Century Resort*: This is my personal favorite, and is the resort I stayed at. A child who loves numbers, letters, and reading will love it here. Oldies music softly fills the air. Each building represents a different decade of the century, and the slang of the era is written on the building. The years of the century are scrolled everywhere. This resort actually teaches children language and 20th century culture. The pools are seasonally heated and have great sight lines. It is on a lake with the Generation Gap Bridge extending across it. When I was there, no water recreational facilities had been built on the lake.

The Moderate Resorts

These resorts border bodies of water and offer a greater variety of activities, pools, and play areas for the children than the other resorts do. The landscaping and decorations are of finer detail. The pools are not fenced in. There are more choices of eating establishments, including some sit-down restaurants.

- *Caribbean Beach:* The buildings at this resort are themed around the different islands of the Caribbean. There is a beautiful white-sand beach on a lagoon. Six heated pools dot the area. The feature pool is at Olde Port Royale; it has water slides, shooting water cannon, and waterfalls. Parrot Cay Island is a one-acre play area in the middle of the lake, featuring narrow paths, parrots, and a playground area. Boat and bike rentals are available. Some rooms have beds with posts that could be snapped, and your child might also show some interest in certain light fixtures and chairs. The landscaping is good, and offers few places to hide. Restaurants include Shutters—a fine dining establishment with American and Caribbean cuisine—and the Market Street Food Court for quick family fare.

- *Coronado Springs:* A sprawling, Mexican-themed resort around a large lake. It includes the Mayan Dig Site play area. The main pool has a large Mayan pyramid with water flowing down it. Children can climb up the steps of the pyramid. They are blocked from going too high by large tree roots. My concern is that the tree roots may not deter a child with autism. I had to stay away from pools when Nicky was young because of his persistent attempts to reach the deep end. A persistent child with autism could wear a parent out as they try to keep him off that pyramid. Most of the other amenities at this resort revolve around convention-goers.

- *Port Orleans—Riverside:* Dense vegetation surrounds this resort. Do not take a child who is a flight risk here. You could lose him in the underbrush in seconds. The furniture in the Alligator Bayou buildings is rustic and made from sticks. This could pose a problem for children who like to play with sticks. The furniture at the Magnolia Bend buildings looks sturdier, the chairs being a mild concern. The amenities include an old-time water hole with a slide on Ol' Man Island (there are some sight line issues at the pool area), horse-drawn carriages, and fishing (catch and release) along the Sassagoula River. Restaurants include Riverside Mill, featuring Cajun cuisine, Sassagoula Pizza Express for family fare, and the Boatwright Dining Hall featuring Southern and other American cuisine.

- *Port Orleans—French Quarter:* This is a sister resort to Riverside. It is themed after the beautiful streets of New Orleans with wrought iron balconies and cobblestone streets. The balconies may be attractive to a climber. The furniture is sturdy. My only concern is that the latticework in the corners of the room may prove attractive to a child who likes sticks. There is a pool with a dragon water-slide with some sight-line issues, fishing (catch and release), as well as boat and bike rentals. This resort shares the Ol' Man Island play area with Riverside. It also shares the Boatwright Dining Hall, which features Southern and other American cuisine, and the Sassagoula Pizza Express. The Sassagoula Floatworks and Food Factory offers quick family fare.

The Deluxe Resorts

These resorts offer luxurious accommodations, children's clubs, concierge services, business facilities, gourmet restaurants, and unique recreational opportunities. If you intend to enroll your child, contact the children's club well before you visit. Discuss your child's supervision needs and abilities. Guest Services always tries to accommodate, but intense needs or short notice can pose problems. Some of the rooms have private balconies. You should move the furniture inside if you have concerns about your child trying to scale the balcony. The pool areas are often only partially fenced in. Scout the exterior. Openings can occur, especially near the maintenance areas.

- *Animal Kingdom Lodge:* Sit on your balcony and watch giraffes eating just a few feet away from you. This beautiful resort borders the African savannah of the Animal Kingdom. There is a zoo area at the resort where you can watch the animals being fed. The African thatched-hut architecture completes the setting. There is a working fireplace in the lobby with high screens around it, but a determined child could throw something over them. The African-style furniture in the rooms is sturdy, but some of the wall hangings and lamps may prove attractive. Ask to have them removed if you are concerned. The tempting ceiling fans have to stay. There is a massage and fitness center for adults, and Simba's Club and the Hakuna Matata playground for the children. The outdoor pool is zero-level entry (no steps), and is surrounded by lush foliage and rocks. It is very romantic, but if you were looking for a lost child, it would be impossible. The outdoor pool includes a 67-foot slide. Restaurants include Jiko—the Cooking Place, and Boma—Flavors of Africa, which feature African and other international cuisines. Mara serves quick family fare.

- *Beach Club Resort:* This resort is themed after Victorian Cape May and has wooden seaside houses, gardens, cabanas, and croquet and tennis courts. There are outdoor pools, white-sand beaches, and boat rentals at the marina. The wrought-iron furniture is sturdy. The rooms have slats on the closet doors that may be tempting to a child who loves sticks. The Ship Shape Health Club is for the adults, and the Sandcastle Club is for the children. Walking paths and boardwalks border a large lake that is shared with several other resorts. These resorts share the three-acre Stormalong Bay lakeside water park. It has water slides and pretty good sight lines, despite its unusual shape, but it is only partially gated. There is a fence with a gate that separates this park from the sidewalk that passes by the lake, but if you follow the fence just a few feet around a corner, there is a large opening by the maintenance sheds. Your child could slip out of the pool area if you assume that the fence is complete. Restaurants include the Beaches & Cream Soda Shop and Hurricane Hanna's Grill for light family fare. The Cape May Café serves clams, mussels, chicken, and ribs.

- *BoardWalk Inn:* This resort is a sentimental favorite of mine. It evokes childhood memories of summers at New Jersey beach towns with a boardwalk full of arcade games, T-shirt shops, and especially saltwater taffy. The pool is filled with the amusement park-style pieces associated with the store. The Keister Coaster is a water slide modeled after the wooden roller coasters of the era. The sight lines are partially obscured. The wrought-iron furniture is sturdy. The slatted settee and closet doors may prove a temptation to your child. Amenities include a marina with boat and bike rentals, tennis courts, the Luna Park play area, and the Muscles and Bustles Health Club for adults. It is located near the ESPN Sports Club, which has more than one hundred televisions showing sporting events. Restaurants include Big River Grille and Brewing Works for casual dining, the Flying Fish Café for seafood and steaks, and Spoodles for Mediterranean-style family fare.

- *Contemporary Resort:* This is one of the original Walt Disney World resorts and dates back to the early 1970s. Located along the monorail, it provides quick access to the Magic Kingdom and to Epcot. The main building is an A-frame over the monorail station. Hallway balconies overlook the Grand Canyon Concourse below. Having a child who is a climber, it concerns me that a child could fall or drop an object onto the concrete floor below. The other buildings in the complex are low to the ground and of traditional shape. Stay in one of those if your child is a climber. The furniture in the rooms is sturdy. Amenities include pools, beach, boat rentals, tennis courts, and children's play areas. There is the Olympiad Fitness Center for adults. Dining options include the Food 'n' Fun Center for family-friendly food, Chef Mickey's for buffet dining, as well as the Concourse Steakhouse and the California Grill, which offer fine dining options and feature West Coast cuisine.

- *Grand Floridian:* This is Walt Disney World's flagship resort. It's located across the lake from the Magic Kingdom, with monorail and water taxi service to the theme parks. Amenities include pools, beach, tennis courts, boat rentals, and childcare. The Grand Floridian Spa and Health Club is for the adults, and the Mouseketeer Club is for the children. Special tea parties and pirate cruises are available for the kids. Cooking classes and high-tea parties are available for the adults. Most of the furniture is sturdy; however, the posts on the beds could be a temptation. Dining options abound. Citricos offers fine Mediterranean cuisine. Victoria and Albert's offers very fine, high-service dining. Garden View Tea has high afternoon tea. Norcoossee's specializes in North American seafood. The Grand Floridian Café offers casual dining, and Gasparilla's Grill and Games has family fare.

- *Polynesian Resort:* Another of the original resorts dating back to the 1970s, it is located on the monorail line across from the Magic Kingdom. If you were trying to locate a missing child, the resort's lush foliage could present a problem. The foliage around the pool area disrupts sight lines. The bamboo and wicker furniture is vulnerable to breakage. Amenities include pools, a beach, fishing, and boat rental. Adults have access to the neighboring Grand Floridian Spa and Health Club. Children can enjoy the Neverland Club. Dining options include O'Hana, which features a Polynesian feast grilled over an open fire; Kona Café, which features Asian cuisine, and Captain Cook's Snack and Ice Cream Company for family fare. The Spirit of Aloha Dinner Show is a luau, complete with dancers and fire-eaters.

- *Wilderness Lodge:* The majestic scenery of the Pacific Northwest is on glorious display, complete with totem poles and geysers. Hidden Springs Pool is surrounded by lush vegetation that can interfere with sight lines. The Silver Creek Pool has better visibility. There are white-sand beaches, boat and bike rentals, fishing, hiking, and playgrounds. The Cubs Club is for the children. Chip 'n' Dale hold nightly campfire sing-a-longs. The furniture in the rooms is very breakable, because everything is done with slats. There is a fireplace in the lobby. Dining options include Artist's Point for Pacific Northwest cuisine. Whispering Canyon Café for western lodge fare of smoked and barbequed food, and Roaring Fork Snacks for family fare.

- *Yacht Club:* This resort has all the elegance of a fine New England yacht club. Breakables abound throughout the lobby. There is even a full china cabinet in one of the halls. The furniture looks sturdy, but the slatted headboards could pose a temptation for children with autism. Amenities include pools, a white-sand beach, boardwalks, piers leading to a lighthouse, and boat rentals. It shares Stormalong Bay water-park with the Beach Club. The water park's sight lines are good, considering the odd shape; however, it is only partially fenced in. There are gaps in the fence by the maintenance sheds where a child could slip away from the pool area. The Ship Shape Health Club is for adults; the Sandcastle Club is for children. Both these facilities are shared with guests from the Beach Club. Dining options include the Yachtsman Steakhouse and the Yacht Club Gallery, both of which feature American cuisine. Family fare is available at Hurricane Hanna's Grill at the neighboring Beach Club.

The Vacation Club Resorts

Many years ago, we bought a timeshare not associated with Disney. It has been wonderful for traveling with children who have autism, because it provides a homelike environment, with separate bedrooms and a fully stocked kitchen where I can cook their favorite foods. Many come with full laundry facilities and whirlpool baths. Multiple bedrooms allow for a larger number of guests (helpers!) to stay with the family. Disney developed these vacation villas to appeal to the timeshare crowd. If you wish to buy into the plan, please contact Disney for details. I am reviewing accommodations that I have viewed only over the Internet. It is, of necessity, an incomplete view. Breakables can usually be hidden away in closets.

- *Beach Club Villas:* This resort shares all the amenities of the Beach Club. Please see that section for more details. Room sizes vary from a studio that sleeps four to a two-bedroom that sleeps eight, complete with kitchen.

- *BoardWalk Villas:* This resort shares all the amenities of the BoardWalk Club. Please see that section for more details. Room sizes vary from a studio that sleeps four, to a three-bedroom that sleeps twelve. Most of the furniture seems sturdy, but the kitchen chairs have slats.

- *Old Key West Resort:* This resort was built for Vacation Club members. It recreates turn-of-the century Key West with gingerbread-accented Victorian homes. Amenities include pools, playground, basketball courts, a marina, and a nearby golf course. The R.E.S.T. Beach Recreation Department stands for Recreation, Exercise, Swimming, and Tennis. Dining options include Olivia's Cafe, which features American food, and Good's Food to Go, which features family fare take-out. Room sizes vary from studios that sleep four, to three-bedrooms that sleep twelve. The furniture includes slatted cabinets and woodwork and a room filled with venetian blinds.

- *Saratoga Springs:* This resort is themed after the elegant resorts of the Adirondacks in New York. The furniture in the three-bedroom deluxe suite is elegant and expensive. The furniture in the smaller suites appears sturdy. Posts on the beds may prove attractive. Amenities include High Rock Spring pool, which has grottos and waterfalls (some sight line issues), The Spa for adults, Lake Buena Vista golf course, children's playgrounds, horseback riding, and tennis and basketball courts. The Artist's Palette is a self-serve restaurant with salads, soups, pizza, and other family fare.

- *The Villas at Wilderness Lodge:* This resort shares all the amenities of the Wilderness Lodge. Please see that section for more details. Room sizes vary from a studio that sleeps four, to a two-bedroom that sleeps eight. The furniture appears sturdy, but has some slat-work.

Cabins and Campgrounds

- *Fort Wilderness Resort and Campground:* This is a beautiful area with meadows, trees, and a lake. The cabins with a full kitchen create a homelike setting. The rustic furniture does resemble sticks, and identical-looking cabins may cause confusion. Amenities include pools, white-sand beach horseback riding, a petting farm, pony rides, hayrides, and carriage rides. Dining options are Mickey's Backyard BBQ, and Trail's End Restaurant for a family fare buffet. The Hoop Dee Doo Musical Revue provides all-you-can-eat country cooking and foot-stomping entertainment.

Part Five

The Anheuser-Busch Family of Theme Parks

Sea World and Busch Gardens Tampa Bay are interesting places to take children with autism. The animal and marine life portions of the parks are excellent, even for the low-functioning child. On the other hand, the rides are usually intense coasters that are too much even for a high-functioning child. I have had issues with Guest Relations at these parks. Hopefully, you will find them more cooperative.

Disability passes are not going to be as helpful at these parks as at the theme parks. Most of the rides with lines are for the roller coasters, which your child will probably not want to ride. Get the passes, but also pay extra for the Quick Queue option that will speed you through those lines and back to your family.

Chapter 23

Sea World

Sea World is a great park for a child with autism. Most of the park involves watching and interacting with marine life at your own pace. Your family should enjoy this park. When I was there in December of 2003, I felt that the staff had little or no understanding of what a parent who has children with autism is up against. I was told several times that I could not see the marine life without seeing a film first. I have written about ways to get around that. I am not one to advocate insubordination, but my belief is that the management would have been horrified to learn that a disabled child had been turned away from an exhibit when a short trip up the exit ramp could have corrected the problem.

- *The Lighthouse:* This is a good place to preoccupy a child with autism while the rest of the family gets their tickets and goes through security.

- *Dolphin Nursery:* A wonderful viewing area of mother dolphins and their new offspring.

- *Seaport Theater:* See an amusing pet show called "Pets Ahoy." Your child should enjoy this if he can sit through a show.

- *Tropical Reef:* This building shelters huge aquariums of fish and other sea life found on a tropical reef. The contrast between the bright sunlight outside and the relative darkness inside may mildly disturb a child with autism, but observing fish can be a fascinating activity for children.

- *Tide Pool:* This exhibit provides an outdoor look at the water life to be found in tidal pools. My child wanted to splash his hands in that water and touch the marine life, but it is not healthy for the fish. I recommend this area.

- *Turtle Point:* Your child should enjoy this exhibit.

- *Stingray Lagoon:* This is a tank where your child can splash his hands to his heart's content, and touch the stingrays as they swim by. The look on your child's face when he accidentally touches one is priceless.

- *Dolphin Cove:* In this wonderful area, you can see the dolphins play and swim in a natural habitat. The underwater viewing area was a tremendous hit with my children!

- *Key West Dolphin Stadium:* Your child should like the animal portions of this show. Low-functioning children tend to lose patience when the dolphin trainers are speaking. Station yourself near the end of an aisle for easy exiting. Avoid the splash zone.

- *Manatees—The Last Generation?:* There is a short film (five minutes?) about manatees before viewing the animals. Go up the exit to see the animals if your child can't sit through a show. Manatees are slow-moving creatures that float just below the water's surface. Your child may not be too interested in them.

- *Journey to Atlantis:* This is a steep flume ride—only for children already comfortable with flume rides. Be sure to see the Jewels of the Sea Aquarium in the gift shop as you leave.

- *Jewels of the Sea Aquarium:* Look at the ceiling in the entrance to the Golden Sea Horse Gift Shop. You will see the Aquarium above you! I had trouble getting my low-functioning child to look up. There are also smaller aquariums in the walls, and even underneath a clear floor.

- *Kraken:* This intense, floorless roller coaster is not recommended for children with autism. Only a roller coaster addict should ride this one.

- *Manta:* For this roller coaster, you ride lying down with your face toward the ground. It is meant to simulate flying. You also skim the water's surface. This is a very cool ride, but only for your roller coaster fanatic.

- *Penguin Encounter:* This is a cool place in more ways than one. This trip to Antarctica to view the different types of penguins is especially enjoyable on a hot day. I recommend this exhibit.

- *Pacific Point Reserve:* A terrific area for walking around and viewing the seals and sea lions. They can get very noisy. Feed the sea lions if your child will tolerate it.

- *Sea Lion and Otter Stadium:* See a silly show called "Clyde and Seymour Take Pirate Island." Your child should enjoy it if he can sit through the show. Prepare yourself for lots of puns and slapstick humor.

- *Shark Encounter:* Do not miss this adventure! You walk through a large shark tank inside a glass hallway. A low-functioning child may just continue to walk quickly through this exhibit, but so long as they see that there is someplace they can head to, they usually cope.

- *Nautilus Theater:* Odyssea is an acrobatic show with an underwater setting. The enjoyment level depends on whether your child has an interest in the production. Early parts of the show include audience interaction.

- *Clydesdale Hamlet:* The Anheuser-Busch Clydesdales are on display in the paddock or in their stables.

- *Anheuser-Busch Hospitality Center:* A place to get food and beer. There is a small area describing the brewing process.

- *Splash Attack Game:* This attraction is near a children's play area that requires tokens for some activities.

- *Wild Arctic:* Be sure to see the walruses, polar bears, and whales. They can be viewed after seeing a film and taking an optional helicopter trip. If your child is low-functioning and can't sit through a show, go in through the exit in the gift shop. The film of the arctic is beautiful. To get to the research station, you can either take the hiking route or the helicopter simulator ride. There are height requirements for the helicopter ride. Low-functioning children may find it too intense.

- *Shamu Stadium:* This is the house that Shamu built. A low-functioning child may lose patience during the long stretches when the trainer is speaking. Between shows, take low-functioning children to see the whales at the underwater viewing area.

- *Sky Tower:* Low-functioning children enjoy the view and the ride up. It does cost extra. You might want to try this ride near the end of your visit, so you can point out all the things you've seen that day.

- *Discovery Cove:* I have not been there. From the brochure, it looks like it would be fabulous if your child is able to snorkel. A limited number of people swim and snorkel around dolphins and tropical fish. There are free-flight aviaries with tropical birds flying around you. I hope to be able to do this someday.

Chapter 24

Busch Gardens, Tampa Bay

Tampa Bay's Busch Gardens are to the west of the Orlando/Lake Buena Vista theme-park hub. It has the best children's play area, and there are plenty of animals to view. A major drawback to the park is that many of their roller coasters roar. This may make children with sound sensitivities shy away from certain sections of the park.

I would love to give you a detailed layout of all the animal exhibits as well as the rides, but my son ate the park map with my notes on it. A requested new map from Busch Gardens was never received, so I am using the Internet map, which has less detail. The second edition will have more detailed information.

- *Morocco:* The entrance to Busch Gardens immediately transports you into an exotic world reminiscent of Arabian Nights. Many small shops fill this area, including Sultan's Sweets. This bake-shop is a regular stop on our trip. You can sit out in the bazaar and watch shows. I believe that the Desert Grill, which offers more substantial food, is also here. Your child needs to have some restaurant experience for this restaurant.

- *KaTonga:* This is a new show about aspiring African storytellers who perform with puppets, music, and dance. Language comprehension issues associated with autism will impair the child's

99

ability to understand the stories, but a high-functioning child may enjoy the spectacle. A low-functioning child with many sensory issues is likely to be over-stimulated.

- *Gwazi:* This giant, double, wooden roller coaster twists and turns in on itself and out again. The ride and the associated noise are too intense for a child with autism.

Egypt

To the right of Morocco is Egypt. On the way there, stop and see the Clydesdale horses at Clydesdale Hamlet. They are a special feature at all Anheuser-Busch theme parks.

- *Montu:* This ride dominates the area of Egypt. Do not stand by the archway to Egypt, because it looks like the people on the Montu are headed straight for you. It terrified my children, who had no way of knowing that the people were going to curl back away from them. Stand a little to the side, so they do not get a head-on view. Noise levels can be an issue with this ride. It helps if you stand outside the archway and look into the shops.

- *King Tut's Tomb:* This is a reproduction of the 1920s excavation site of King Tut's tomb. There is a play area for kids to do their own digging.

- *Serengeti Plain:* Across from Egypt, you will see the Crown Colony. This restaurant has panoramic views of the Serengeti Plain with full table service and an upscale menu. The child should have a high level of "restaurant savvy" before entering here. The views from the restaurant are just one of the many ways to enjoy the animals and views of the Serengeti.

- *Edge of Africa:* This is a self-guided walking tour, allowing you to view many of the African animals. My children loved this. It gave them a chance to explore and control their own pace. Be sure to take pictures that you can turn into flashcards at a later time.

- *The Skyride:* This gentle, enclosed cable-car ride is located to the left of the Crown Colony. Your family can view the spectacular scenery as you float over the park to the Congo area.

Myombe Reserve

If you choose not to take the Skyride to the Congo area, turn toward the left as you pass it to get to Myombe Reserve. This is the home of the Great Apes. It is my favorite place in the park.

Nairobi

After you leave the Myombe Reserve, you will find yourself in Nairobi, with more opportunities to explore the Serengeti Plain.

- *Serengeti Railway:* This is the easiest way for a low-functioning child to view the African Plain. The round-trip train ride takes you through the Serengeti and other parts of the park. The other train stations were closed for renovations when I was there.
- *Rhino Rally:* An off-road jeep tour that gets you close to the animals but also plunges you into adventurous driving situations. A low-functioning child may have some difficulty with noise and jostling.
- *Serengeti Safari:* This safari trip is appropriate for everyone. It's mostly a "show and tell" attraction.

Timbuktu

After you leave Nairobi, head out to Timbuktu. This part is pure amusement park rides. There are more attractions here than I am listing. Unfortunately, without my map with notes, I can only comment on the major ones. The others are types that you may already be familiar with.

- *Scorpion:* A roller coaster with a 60-foot drop and a 360-degree loop. Some children with autism really love roller coasters and become roller coaster addicts. If your child already loves roller coasters, this one is okay. Skip it if he has never been on a roller coaster, or has been on them but remains unsure about them.

- *Cheetah Chase:* This new mini-coaster is five stories high and full of small drops and tight turns. A high-functioning child should enjoy it, and I might even try a ride-savvy, low-functioning child on it. Your judgment should be based on how he has handled other rides of similar excitement level, and whether there are issues with heights or panic. The child has to be forty-six inches tall, and at least six years old to ride it.

- *Sesame Street 4-D:* This is not recommended for low-functioning children with autism. They do not like 3-D movies. They prefer that the characters stay on the screen. The 4-D multi-sensory surprises maybe too much for some children with autism.

Congo

This is the deepest part of Africa, and The Skyride ends here as well. It is also home to the noisiest roller coaster in the park. The roars of Kumba, the roller coaster, surround you. A child with sound sensitivities may want to hurry by or avoid the area entirely. Be sensitive to what may be the problem if you find the child is getting distressed. Understand that children with autism sometimes struggle with filtering out background noise.

- *Congo River Rapids:* This is a whitewater, twelve-person raft ride. You can try this if your high-functioning child has already been on raft rides and is all right with them. I would start a low-functioning child on a raft ride at a water park that does not have the added stimulation of geysers, waterfalls, and other ominous scenery.

- *Jungala:* It is a beautiful spot to see the rare white tigers and other cats.

Stanleyville

Be sure to see the rare white tigers and other cats between Congo and Stanleyville. It is a beautiful spot in the midst of all the high excitement rides of Stanleyville. You might want to consider changing your child into swim-clothes or having a change of clothes available before going on the water rides. Some children have no compunction about stripping off wet clothing.

- *Stanley Falls:* A log flume ride that a high-functioning child could really enjoy, provided he doesn't mind getting wet—er, make that "soaked."
- *Tanganyika Tidal Wave:* This is a tranquil river ride until you go over a 55-foot drop at the end. Everyone in the raft—and those watching the raft from the sidewalks—gets soaked.
- *Python:* This would be good for a roller coaster addict, but it's too much for most children with autism. You go through a double, spiraling corkscrew and a 70-foot drop.
- *SheiKra:* It's a diving roller coaster that is too intense for children with autism.

Land of Dragons

This is the best children's play area in any of the parks. A valued feature, from an autism perspective, is that there is only one way in and out, and that it is surrounded by netting. There is a mixture of attractions, all of which a child with autism would find appealing.

There is a dragon splash area for children who love to play in water, a three-story tree house with paths of rope mesh for exploring and a small play area with slides and other things to climb on. We have spent many enjoyable times here.

Bird Gardens

Head over to the Bird Gardens for a slower pace. Walk through enclosed aviaries with hundreds of birds surrounding you. Even the low-functioning children should enjoy the bird areas.

- *Lory Landing:* It is a walk-through area that has parrots and lorikeets.
- *Sesame Street Safari of Fun:* It is a wonderful play area for the children. There is also a show with the Sesame Street characters.
- *Walkabout Way:* This is a great place for visiting our animal friends from Down Under. The kids should enjoy it.

Afterword

As you can tell, we've been many places with our children. We have had good experiences and "Let's not do *that* again!" experiences, but they were all precious. I know you will come away with treasured memories, too.

Good luck—and I hope to see you in Florida!

Resources

AAA
www.aaa.com

Amtrak
1.800.872.7245
www.amtrak.com

Busch Gardens, Tampa Bay
888.800.5447
www.buschgardens.com/buschgardens/fla

Disney World
407.034.7639
www.disney.go.com

Sea World
800.327.2424
www.seaworld.com/seaworld/fla

Universal Studios
407.363.8000
www.universalorlando.com

Index

About the Author

Kathy Labosh graduated from Penn State and worked as an economist. She is now a stay-at-home mom to Sam and Nicky, both of whom are children with autism. It became her mission to help others in similar situations.

Kathy formed a Special Education Religion Class and is the author of a specialized curriculum for children with autism. She also received an Honorable Mention for Children's Fiction from *Writer's Digest*.

Kathy continues to work on additional books in The Child with Autism series, including *The Child with Autism at Home and in the Community* (2011), *The Child with Autism Learns about Faith* (2011), and *The Child with Autism Learns MORE about Faith* (still in progress).

Be sure to check out more titles in The Child with Autism series!

This book epitomizes the value of the phrase "been there, done that!" In this amazingly helpful guide for family members, friends, and professionals, author and mom Kathy Labosh and special-educator LaNita Miller take on the issues and obstacles that parents and educators face every day. Hundreds of easy-to-read bullet points provide tips that readers can put into action immediately. First they cleverly tackle home life, from breakfast to bedtime, and then they take readers on a trip through the community, offering essential do's and don'ts for going to restaurants, church, the doctor's, the grocery store, family gatherings, and more! With Kathy and LaNita's insight and advice, you can be better prepared for the unique challenges autism throws your way!
978-1-935274-20-9
$14.95

Children with autism CAN learn about God! Endorsed by religious leaders, this groundbreaking book offers a step-by-step lesson plan for family members, educators, and church staff—including scripted narratives, group activities, prayers, scripture readings, classroom setup guidance, lists of additional resources, and more. Each lesson is also accompanied by a Scripture Study for instructors to help them prepare for each class, where the author provides additional ideas and discussion questions. Students will learn about: Creation, Adam and Eve, Temptation, Cain and Abel, Noah, Abraham, Isaac and Rebekah, Jacob, Joseph, Moses, and Passover. And the book teaches parents and teachers about: Autism Ministry, Class Setup, How Kids Learn, How to Prepare, How to Teach, and more!
978-1-935274-19-3
$14.95

CPSIA information can be obtained at www.ICGtesting.com
263876BV00001B/1/P